THE PURSUIT OF PATIENCE

The Pursuit of Patience

Understanding our pursuit to live a life with lasting patience

MICHELLE SMIC

Smic Life smiclife.com

Copyright © 2021 by Team Smic Pty Ltd
Southbrook, Qld AUSTRALIA
www.smiclife.com

All rights reserved. No part of this publication may be reproduced in any form, stored in a retrieval system, or transmitted in any form or by any means – for example by any electronic, recording, photocopying or mechanical means including information storage and retrieval systems, without the prior written permission of Team Smic Pty Ltd. The only exception is brief quotations in printed reviews.

This publication is intended to provide helpful and informative material in regard to the subject matter. It is sold with the understanding that the Author and Team Smic Pty Ltd expressly disclaim responsibility for any adverse effects arising from the application or use of any advice or information contained in this publication.

This book is not intended as a substitute for medical advice from a qualified physician. The intent of this book is to provide general information in regard to the subject matter covered. Readers should consult their personal health professional before adopting any of the suggestions or be influenced by anything in this book. If medical advice or other expert help is needed, the services of an appropriate medical professional should be sought.

Cover photo by Dwayne Mason
Cover & interior design by Michelle Smic

ISBN TP: 9780645187526
ISBN eBook: 9780645187533
FIRST EDITION

This book is dedicated to FAQ, and Kylie. Thank you for helping me, showing me and giving me a greater understanding of patience. You helped me trust myself in relation to others, so I can trust others.

Thank you for helping me find my voice and my feet. Thank you for showing me a better way to live and my place in this world.
Thank you for believing in me.

Contents

About The Author ix

Introduction 1

1
UNITY

1	Relative	8
2	Community	15
3	Process	25
4	Connection	37
5	Understanding Unity	43

2
COMPASSION

| 6 | Compassionate | 54 |
| 7 | Unique | 61 |

8	Boundries	71
9	Communication	86
10	Understanding Compassion	102

3
PERSEVERANCE

11	Persevere	114
12	Ambition	120
13	Priorities	133
14	Purpose	141
15	Understanding Perseverance	146

References 153

My desire for writing this book is not for you to know and memories this book from the front to the back, but for you to understand my intention for it. It's only when you understand my intention for these books that they can actually have a positive effect on your life. It's only when these theories and ideas are implemented into your life that you will start to understand the freedom that I have and the freedom that I want to share with you.

This book is a book of my own ideas and theories. I have no doctrine or PHD, just a wealth of life experience, a bible, my friends, and community. All that I have learnt has come from living, learning, and loving through the shame and doubt.

Through my journey, I have definitely struggled with patience, but maybe not in the way you may think. My struggle with patience has been that I may have had too much of it.
My life has been riddled with trusting people who displayed qualities affirming that I had trust issues. In my endeavour to see the best in people I scarified my own needs to accommodate and excuse others. This led to relationships without boundaries and decisions based on which one would hurt someone else less.

Then when I found myself, I found how to trust myself and discovered my voice, I then feared losing it again. I pushed away relationships and people because I didn't believe we could be friends or hold deep conversations if we didn't believe the same thing or do the same thing.
I thought that there had to be something wrong with one of us to have different views.
Conversations with other people would cause me to doubt my own belief. I didn't want to doubt because I didn't want to question.

I had noticed I was different, but for the first time it had been a good thing.

I will never have everything in common with one person and I also believe I have something in common with every person. Being different wasn't that scary but developing relationships with people knowing this was hard. I left a lot of my old friends behind. The one's who had supported me and been there for me. I looked for friends who could have deep conversations were the aim wasn't to convince but to learn.

Questions become the source of most conversations with my willingness to learn. The issue is that some people start to get suspicious when I asked a lot of questions. Especially if they were questions, they were not willing to ask themselves.

My patience has really been tested with my relationships with the people I hold most dear. My aim was to keep forgiving them, to show them love. This led to them walking all over me, sometimes literally.

When I changed the purpose of my relationships to building trust in people. I learnt a lot about relationships through the reactions to my change of behaviour. Not everyone is going to accept change straight away, but I trust in this method and am taking the time to really consider my own intentions for my relationships. I know they are pure; I know they are good, but I also know I am not perfect and that not everyone is on the same journey. I endeavour to learn more about who they are and what they need, I am able to fill those needs consistently and with boundaries to establish a relationship, based on the premise of continual learning. That is learning more about each other and out effect as the time goes by. Knowing there will never be a point in time I will know them completely but looking forward to discovering more.

I have both loved it and hated writing this book, as I cannot write what I do not know. After completing the first draft, I had about ten days of intense learning and a real need for patience, so I scraped that edition and started again with a renewed perspective. Then came the third perspective of patience. The more we practice these traits of learning and accepting, the more we grow. We need not despise the growth of our patience any more than we despise the depth of our connections.

I hope that you take joy and privilege in both.

Introduction

This book is the second in the series 'Minds Work'.

I recommend that you do read the complete series to understand the full concept and how it can be applied to life. The first book 'Thinking for Yourself', and after this book, keep an eye out for Book three, 'An Appetite of Appreciation'.

These will help build our life, love and purpose in the world on a firm foundation. The first book is designed to help you work on yourself, to understand what is really going on in your head and heart.

Throughout this book I use the terms experience and exposure. To clarify these:

Experience = (Knowledge or practical wisdom gained from what one has observed, encountered, or undergone.)
A thought, feeling or action that we have experienced either through generations or our life. This is personal experience involving a situation where our choices resulted in the outcome. eg. The conversation we had yesterday or the gesture that we made to another person.

Exposure = (Presentation to view, especially in an open or public manner)
An event or situation where we were not directly involved, and our decisions had no effect on the outcome of the situation, eg. Films or dramas, or maybe the latest news story.

We can feel compassion in the situation of exposure and guilt in the situation of experience.

It is important to understand and note the difference of these terms, especially in an environment with other people.

This book is about discovering our patience.

Patience is only needed within community and connections. Without interaction with other people, there would be no need to hurry or the keeping of time. It's only through expectations, that patience is needed.

When we come together as a community, understand our fellow human and enjoy in our lives, then patience will find its perfect place.

No matter how much peace and self-control we have, without community and a sharing of our experiences, we will never have patience. It may be easier if we start at the start because I've found that it's always the best place to start.

What is the purpose of patience?

The purpose of patience is to enjoy the journey. To dread life is to defeat the purpose of breathing. We come into and leave this life with nothing, with each breath we can laugh, or we can cry, we can love or hate, and we can enjoy or protect.

Patience is action.

Patience is expressed through working with other people. Working with others is much easier when we can understand ourselves. Understanding others comes from understanding our own intensions and desires.

We are all inherently the same, born with the same needs and deep desires.

At a very base level, we are all made the same, created differently through our experiences and exposures, and assume different reasons and purposes.

We all offer something totally unique to the world.

The things that I struggle with, I have seen others struggle with too. We are not the first ones, and we won't be the last. Feeling disconnected and alone doesn't mean that no one understands, it just means we're not talking to them. There is someone that can help us through, this usually as happens as we help them through something too.

You can't get Patience.

Despite the title of this book, I don't believe that patience is something you can get. In my experience chasing it usually results in chasing it away. That being said, patience is something you find and discover, through interaction with other people.

You can't have patience; you have to be patient.

To be patient, we first have to be confident in who we are. This comes by know that we are learning, just like everyone else. True confidence is confidence in the good and in the learning. This is why 'Thinking for Yourself' is an important first step.

Striving for or putting pressure on myself to be more patient can have the opposite effect.

Being patient comes through relationships.

I can be very, very patient sitting on a hill by myself, with no expectations or tasks to complete. Without interaction or conversing with other people, I never have an issue with patience.

When I add just one person into the situation, things change. I find myself having to stop and listen or explain and co-operate and maybe 'waste time' gaining understanding.

Patience is found in the search of understanding others.

We all have patience on some level, because we all have an understanding of other people on some level. As any skill, it needs to be practised and developed. The only way this can happen is by building it together with the people around us.

In this book, I attempt to explain patience as a more wholistic search for joy.

While discovering healthier relationships by exercising the application of patience in the presence of community. I have found the added benefit of finding patience is that we also find joy, where we no longer despise any part of our lives but enjoy it.

Thinking for ourselves is just the start, as now we can establish relationships that encourage others to think for themselves.

Patience is allowing others to walk their own path while still creating and maintaining relationships. Patience is something we seek because we all desire relationships and connection.
Relationship without patience is hard and draining.
Relationships with patience is enjoyable and inspiring.

We can't exercise patience without relationships.

I also believe we can't have true joy without relationships.
The enjoyment of life is only experienced in the presence of others and within relationships.

If we think about a time that we were exceedingly happy or joyful, we were probably not alone? I would go as far to say that we were definitely not alone in location and mind. If you have experienced true joy, evident by an abundance of energy, without relation to any other person, I would love to hear from you, because in all my experience, it is at the point of sharing that laughter grows

I don't know all the answers, I can only learn from what I have experienced. I have found that even when you have experienced joy by yourself, it usually comes from memories or a reminder of a moment that you shared with someone else or the anticipation of sharing a story or moment with someone else in the future.

Patience is exercised by having the desire for something but not having the immediate opportunity to obtain it.

When we see a need for patience, we can choose to either throw away our desire and the things that make us unique, or we can keep our desires and trust that an opportunity will come at the best time to attain it.

This is our choice, which one do you think is the easiest option?

Growth is found in the joy of learning.

1

Unity

Knowing people are good, intelligent, and trustworthy.

Chapter 1

Relative

We are not in this alone.

Anything and everything that we do as individuals' affects other people and we do it because we are affected by other people.

We were all raised by someone and had decisions made for us in the early stages of life. We are inter-dependent beings. We cannot survive if we attempt to do life alone, we are not designed that way. We are designed to relate to those around us; to live with people and interact with others.

We were all babies at one stage.

As babies we would not have survived without connection to a caregiver. Someone to provide us with food and warmth, but it is so much more than that. It is well researched that children who do not receive the physical touch or affection needed, have difficulties learning and communicating later in life.

Relating, even if only two people can give us the energy to go on.

Years ago, I remember hearing on the news about a young girl held captive for many years by a man who used her for his pleasure. During nearly a decade of isolation, she had a child. While watching an interview with her, she remarked on how her life changed when she had a baby. I noted how her motherly instincts had kicked in and I could see and hear the deep love for her child. This child, despite all the odds, was raised with scarcity of so many things. I noticed how she had survived because of the incredible connection she had with her mother. This child also gave a reason for the mother to go on.

"It takes a village to raise a child."

This African proverb is found true in research of children who are raised within a community environment, they are more adaptable and well rounded. This occurs because they have been exposed to a wider variety of people and beliefs, while still having a caregiver help them interpret the world they see. This happens by building trust in their beliefs, their caregiver and in people.

People raised with a restricted view of the world as a child, will find it harder to trust themselves and the people around them as they mature. This is due to the limited exposure and experiences they have received. Finding it harder to equip themselves to handle different situations.

We don't need to teach our children a list of rules and ways to behave. We simply need to help them to trust their understanding while allowing it to grow.

I see this parallel to solving a maths equation. When learning maths, we don't have to memories every sum to answer every answer. We simply need to learn plus, minus, multiplication, and divide. The rest is understanding the application of these workings.

When a child is able to trust themselves, the rest is understanding the application of this skill through relationships.

The best place to build relationships is with people we already relate to.
When nurtured from birth it is not a matter of establishing but encouraging this understanding to grow. Babies are

born with trust built in, this trust will remain as long as it is nurtured and valued.

Nurtured through questioning.
Valued through answering.

Learning any skill only comes through practice.

The building of trust within a relationship is a process of learning to notice, value and invest in the opportunities we have. Trust is broken when we don't notice, value or invest in it, but all is not lost. Trust also grows through the acknowledgement of the break and deliberate reconnection of unity.

Knowing who we are and how our minds work, can only help us if our intention is to trust others. If we only have an intention to trust ourselves, we will be left second guessing our every thought as we tend to view the world as if it is us against them.

Our experiences through relating.

We learn from and observe relationships and connections to gain exposure of different environments and circumstances. This develops our awareness of the impact of relationships. If our exposure to relationships has not been one of trust, we will not know or understand how trusting relationships work.

Trust being built through questions.

A two-year old can start the process of trusting their own voice and thoughts. This is often labelled as "The terrible twos". This has to do with the development of the mind; their ability to question and their ability to trust. It may be that children who have a strong trust connection are able to ask questions and communicate more effectively. This developing the steady development of self-trust. The other extreme would be that a child has been taught to suppress their uniqueness so profoundly that they do not question anything.

We can only trust to the level we have been trusted.

If we have never had anyone trust us, we will not know how to trust ourselves; if the relationships around us have been fear driven, we will continue to have relationships that are driven by fear, unless we seek to change them. The good news about this is that we are not victims to be pushed or driven but members to be led and guided.

I believe that no one truly hurts anyone on purpose.

Reading the previous statements, it can be easy to blame our parents or caregivers for the way we are raised, but by that standard our caregivers can only blame their caregivers, and so on and so forth. We are all learning, no one of us is perfect, finished or blameless. So, before we go looking for someone to blame, we need to understand that it is our choice to change it or not. If we choose to be the difference, the generations to come will know the difference.

Each one of us is different.

This is why we need each other. This is why there are both male and females. Neither sex is more important or significant then another. Without either, the human race would never survive.

We are all separate beings designed to work together.

If you have ever observed children during parallel play, you will understand how disconnected two people can be while occupying the same space.
Parallel play is a stage of childhood development where toddler aged children play in the same area or similar objects without interaction or communication with each other. While playing with blocks they will build a tower each creating two small towers or they could paint, totally absorbed in their own creation.

They haven't quiet learnt the skill of working together.

All their relationships seem to be either parent-child or the child will dictate or have a protective relationship with a younger child. This is because they have not yet reached a level of trusting themselves, while accepting new information. They do not have the ability to have mutual relationships.

Interacting with others helps us to understand our place in the world.

It's only when children (and people) start to work together and collaborate that those two small block towers, mentioned earlier can become bigger, better and easier.

For more details on trusting yourself, please read 'Thinking for Yourself'.

Chapter 2

Community

Community is needed for wellbeing.

If we don't value the effect we have on other people, we don't truly value who we are and what we can bring to others. We all have an effect on other people, when we value this effect, it can be positive. When we don't value this effect, it's more than likely a negative one.

A changed person can change a family unit, who can change a community, who can change the world. We don't start off thinking that we are going to make this world a better place if our own house has little harmony. If we can't successfully help the ones closest to us, how can we truly help people as a collective.

Trusting those around us will give us a base and support to trust others as a collective.

Trusting the people closest to us is not fearing that they will harm us or hurt us. A positive community is a group of trustworthy people, working together to live a life free from fear.

Living without fear means doing things for others.

A community gives us people to accept and support, knowing that they also accept and support us. When people join together with a common goal, big things can happen. We test our beliefs and form more sustainable beliefs through community.

We need human interaction to grow.

If we don't want to grow in the direction of our community, we will shy away from human interaction. Lack of healthy human interaction is why those of us who had to isolate found it so hard.

Solitary confinement is one of the worst forms of torture, because without interaction with others we struggle to see our effect on the world and therefore our purpose. Without human interaction our life has no meaning. Even monks, who strive to be content while alone and are hesitant to be dependent on anyone or anything, rely heavily on the teachings of those gone before and the donations of others.

It's when our minds are stimulated in a sustainable way that joy comes.

Human interaction can not only stimulate our five senses all at once but stimulates our minds. That is why sitting around a dining table to share a meal can bring so much joy. We have the opportunity to be completely present. We hear, smell, taste, touch and see that we are all working together. We can share our experiences of the past or plan for the future, all a very sub-conscious and innate way that we grow trust for each other by growing together.

Our energy comes from the sharing of who we are and what we are doing.

Those who seek contentment while alone are trying to run on a dying battery. Our energy, whether we like it or not, comes from interactions with others. We need, yes need to find people who think like us to grow. This allows us to share ideas, ask questions and gain a different perspective of the world we live in.

If we don't understand others, we fear them.

If we don't want to understand others, we push them away. Our fear becomes greater than or desire for connection or our need to fulfill our desires. We fear what we do not know or don't want to understand.

Teaching verse learning.

When we learn a new skill from someone, we can expect that they know more than us. We see them as having the answers and they give us the answer. This is the way schools work, a teacher student environment. The teacher/student relationships depict that either I teach you or you teach me.

When we learn about someone, we both grow through the interaction.

New parents teach their babies about life but ask any parent who is willing to grow, and they will tell you how much they have learnt about themselves through the interactions with their child.

Learning through interactions.

Children who parallel play occupy the same space but are unable to collaborate their ideas. The progression from this stage is a milestone as they are learning to collaborate ideas. Being ability to connect and work with others is a vital part of a children's development.
Community gives us another way to learn as we discover together, "what happens if...." This dedication to learning builds trust in relationships through the ability to forgive, learn and grow together.

Learning collaboration.

Similar to the building blocks, your knowledge and my knowledge cannot be as comprehensive as our knowledge. What I have experienced is different to what you have experienced and therefore when our knowledge is shared from our own experiences, we have a greater understanding than we would have if we were to stand alone.

We all have the ability to bring something good to the table.

Yes, questions may make some people feel uncomfortable. Yes, people who used to be able to control us may now get annoyed. People may not value what we have at first because we didn't value it. Value it anyway. Continue to value it and those who also see the value in it will find us as we also value those around us.

We all play a part. We all make our own decisions.

One person cannot rule a community, just like one person cannot change a community. Each person needs the support of other members. Without others who agree or enforce a point of view, the community won't change. A community in agreement is a sustainable one. Each part in a community is of equal importance. When we value the collective decisions more than our own, we expect them to have more authority than we do. We expect them to know more, understand more and edify more than we do.

Hierarchy in order to control.

Valuing other people in our community allows us to value the part we play. When we see one person as more valuable than another, we create a hierarchical way of thinking. We are all of equal worth and purpose, when we choose to value and partake in our purpose the community thrives. When we choose to see ourselves either more important, or (just as damaging) less important than others, the community will never be able to unite completely therefore, not reaching its full potential.

If everyone did what you are doing, would it be a good community?

We all put something into our community, we all partake in life while we breath. Putting good things into the community means good things come out. If we are always wanting something from our community, it is not sustainable. If we always want to give something to our community, we are not sustainable within that community. We can often get annoyed and frustrated at others for not appreciating or validating our actions, yet we often hesitate at taking what the community may be offering. It's a great question to ask yourself, is what I'm doing for the good of all of those around me, or is it just good for me and the people I like?

Bringing something good through our interactions.

We can value ourselves within a community and change the mindset to bring something good to others. Without building a trusting community we will always feel like we are fighting an uphill battle and may try to do it on our own. Through every healthy interaction, everyone's needs are satisfied. Our need to receive is supported by their need to give. Our need to give and have an effect on others is supported by fulfilling their need.

The whole community is more powerful than the sum of the individuals.

Each person plays a part in the direction of their community. When behaviour or ambitions of the group are questionable to one individual, it is up to that individual to ask questions. If questions are not encouraged and the views of one is not supported, it cannot be healthy. We all have the ability to make decisions, when we invest our abilities in an unhealthy community, it becomes more unhealth. Negative changes happen because the power of community amplifies our ability. Positive, sustainable changes can also be amplified through community. Momentum is established and magnified as more people invest in positive change.

Sustainable change requires accountability.

A new mindset can quickly and easily slip away without support. We impact our community as much as our community impacts us. If there wasn't a part for us to play in a community, we wouldn't be in the community. Be aware of the community you keep. Who is changing who, and what are the result of these beliefs being magnified within the community?

Every community can need us, but we don't need every community.

Ever community has a need for people, and we have a need for community. Any community may seem like a perfect match, but we can't let the masses cause us to lose perspective of our own abilities. We need to beware that our need of community does not out way our need for positive connection. Discovering our purpose while finding a community who has a need for that purpose is a more sustainable way to live. It then fills the communities need and the community's purpose is filling our needs. This may take time and we may need to create a platform in which this community can exist.

Without community we have no purpose and without positive purpose, we have no sustainable community.

When we are with people, we are giving something to them, and they are giving something to us. Our purpose is found in our effect on them, and their purpose is found in their effect on us.

Inter-dependence is a mutual reliance on each other.

There is a dependency and independency needed in all communities. There is a sowing and a reaping that needs to occur. This is known as inter-dependence and a final stage of maturity. If we sow anger into an interaction with a sub-conscious person, then we will reap anger from that interaction. If we put good things in, we will get good things out.

As we mature in trusting ourselves, we build the ability to trust in others' intentions.

As we are exposed to and experience different relationships, we are then able to choose what kind of relationships we want to pursue.

A person who has not wanted or appreciated community, has not allowed questioning of their beliefs. Trust is built within community by this questioning, as questioning reveals intension. When intensions are revealed, we can then choose to build trust in mutual positive intentions. A positive community is a good place to question beliefs as it can test to see if it is resounding and sustainable.

Healthy community encourages the journey of learning and does not assume that it is a destination.

Saved by association is not going to give everyone the understanding to grow. Being around good people does not make us a good person unless we see them as an example and have a desire to grow. Wanting to be around someone that we feel has all the answers, does not give us our answers.

Questioning a belief, is a fundamental right to discover who we are and what we choose to believe.

As a community we need to allow people the right to question their beliefs'.

As a community we need to allow people the right to have a difference of opinion.

As a community we need to question peoples doubt in their own beliefs. Questioning, not with the intention to offend as a form of judgment but as a form of bringing clarity to build relationships and understanding.

Chapter 3

Process

The gaining of knowledge isn't our purpose but rather the process of life.

If gaining knowledge was our purpose in life, we would have no need for relationships. Everything we learn, experience and discover on our journeys would end with us. Our life would seemingly be irrelevant as we would not want to exchange information. We would take from others and not give anything back to other people or their lives. If we choose to follow someone else's ideas of life, we would be doing the opposite of what they did by receiving an idea and not contributing our own.

Knowledge is not the key to life, understanding the information we are given can help us to grow.

In the age of information, we have the answers at our fingertips. In our modern day, people have the opportunity to learn a new skill like never before. Thanks to the net, a quick search will find us sifting through mountains of sites or videos looking for the information that is what we want.

Understanding is not evident by knowledge, but by action.

Knowledge is the ability to repeat what we have learnt, to pass a test or to create a plan. Understanding is evident by the application of the information. Only by the questioning or the confirming of the information is the information fully understood and applied to our lives. It is only by the completion of a plan that a plan finds it value. Action without understanding who we are is the following trends, crowds or rule books. We can suppress our unique ability and our genuine self.

Understanding who you are without being able to act on it is torture.

When our desire to fit into a community makes us not want to stand up or stand out, we suppress the very skills and abilities that could enhance the community. When we devalue our deepest needs for the desires of others, we devalue the desires of others by not being willing to contribute to the outcome.

Have you ever been in a situation where you know the answer but are unable to do it or say it?

I'm thinking of doing a puzzle with my two-year-old child. I know exactly where the piece goes and what the puzzle is, but my child insists on trying every other way possible until she finally discovers what is so clear for me to see.

My want is to save time, I want to finish the puzzle and she has the same goal but with different reasoning.

Knowledge is not an asset in this process, understanding is.

Understanding what my purpose is in that moment allows my child to discover her purpose in that moment. My purpose in that moment is not to finish the puzzle or find the answer. My purpose in that moment is to support my child solve the puzzle and discover the answer.

Understanding my purpose in that moment is to understand them.

My desire maybe to finish the puzzle, but my greater desire is to understand what make my child, who they are. Understanding this desire helps me appreciate watching them make mistakes or learn until they discover the answer. My purpose is to encourage them to try again when they lose their patience, to support them in their discovery of their purpose and to celebrate the victory of another freedom achieved.

Knowledge without purpose, is not understanding.

In "Thinking for Yourself" I attempted to help people understand what they are thinking. It gave us a choice to take on a new belief or not. That understanding of what you are thinking is not complete until it includes a discovery of purpose. I don't know whether you changed your beliefs or not, but changing our beliefs is not why we are here.

If gain knowledge was our purpose, then changing our beliefs would be the way.

What is achieved by changing our beliefs' if it has no effect on what we do? It's like watering a plant over and over again and it just doesn't grow. What if too much water makes the plant wilt and become unhealthy? Do we continue to water it?

Thinking for yourself is not the end game.

I am not devaluing the process of discovering who you are or trusting yourself, but this is not where we stop. We can spend our life waiting to be perfect or wanting to know it all before we start doing something, but it's through doing that we discover what we really need. Waiting for our lives to start can be a long process, it can take a lifetime.

We can't remove ourselves from relationships until we learn how to be in them.

This is like taking a stick out of the fire and expecting it to burn as bright. It's expecting us to learn without having the opportunity to understand how relationships work. Removing ourselves from a situation in which we can learn is not going to help us understand. We are not saving ourselves from hurt but prolonging the hurt by protecting ourselves from learning. It is extending the time spent hurting and prolonging the time it takes to learn the skill.

When we remove ourselves from all sources of pain, we remove ourselves from all sources of gain information.

With every trial and hard time comes a need for something to change. When we learn from our experiences, we discover what we need to change. Is it our way of thinking or acting that needs to change? When we can answer that question, we can be open to discovering a different type of relationship and learning a better way of life. With a new way of thinking comes a new habit, with a new habit comes a new way of life.

As we continue to learn, we continue to teach.

As in gardening, there is a time for sowing and a time for reaping. There is a time when we give good things to others and there is a time when we receive from others.

Giving and receiving are both important because without one the other could not exists.

We cannot take anything out of this world. We can only exchange our value with others. Exchanging values for like vales increases the value of both assets. This in turn changes the state of what we have.

If we are only taking from the world and sowing into ourselves, we will only reap from ourselves.

It's a cycle that can be exhausting as it takes energy to keep it moving. A cycle of looking and finding and looking and finding but no growth is achieved. What we find is only what we already have. Our persistence has no purpose if it ends within ourselves. When we take from the world, then the sustainable cycle would be that we give back to the world.

What do we do, if we discover something new?

When we discover something that seems to be new and it has given us freedom and could bring others freedom, we share. That is part of our real purpose, to bring to the world our unique perspective, which is why we are need others.

We need others to share and grow through our experiences, understanding and freedoms. To truly appreciate what we are given, we need to share and grow what we have. Keeping it for ourselves and holding onto it so we don't lose it is to have pride. When pride comes then comes the need to protect or hide what we have; but when we want to learn more, then a greater understanding will come. When we don't want to learn more, we don't allow our understanding to grow. We have learnt from the people before us, whether we like to admit it or not. We don't appreciate what the ones before us have learnt, when we don't appreciate that the ones after us can understand more through us. By acknowledging that we have learnt through our experiences and exposures with others, we own our place in the world by allowing others to learn from us and through the experiences and exposure with them.

We will never survive this life. All we can do is enjoy it in a way that spreads joy.

When suffering is part of life, we don't have to sit in it, we can learn from it. Hard times will come, relationships will be tested. It is through these tests that the relationship builds value. When we are hurt by a friend, and we value that friendship more than the situation that caused hurt, we rebuild and re-establish our friendship with greater understanding of who each of us are. We understand more about their like, dislikes, and needs and they are able learn more about our likes, dislikes and needs.

We know that everyone is learning but not everyone is suffering right now.

Those who love to learn and grow, suffer less. Those who see a moment as an opportunity to learn, share the lesson and not the pain. They decide to change and not resent those who do change or blame others who "made them" change.

Joy is a decision we make.

Joy doesn't just happen; it is a decision that we have to make. When we are presented with joy, we can change it into suffering. When we are presented with suffering, we can change it into finding joy.

I can guarantee joyful people have had their fair share of pain.

They have probably had more than their fair share but have realised that the pain only hurts while we don't want to change. Joy comes through the lesson and after the change. After we let go of our expectations causing the pain, the pain will go. They have also shared in others joy at some stage. Either consciously or sub-consciously, joyful people have learnt through the experiences they have shared with those around them.

The sharing of lessons brings joy.

This helps us to gain perspective in life, we will have times of learning and we may have times of suffering but it's about what we sow into that will multiply. If we are determined not to change our ways when everything around us is changing, our suffering will increase. When we choose to change for the better and accept a better way, even if it is new, we will grow in our joy.

No one's life is perfect just like no one is perfect.

We will all hurt people and we will all be hurt by people. This becomes harder and worst by inviting in guilt and shame. We can either put this on ourselves or others offer it to us. Either way, it doesn't lead to positive growth and joy.

Suppressing our hurt and suffering will not make it go away.

Suppressing will not get rid of anything but allows it to grow unsupervised. It creates a boiling pot of unlearnt lessons, and unresolved problems. If we continually suppress, we continually invest in the hurt and suffering allowing it to multiply until it bursts out at a moment of split focus.

Suppression is not the act that leads to understanding.

Understanding can only come through the revealing of the full situation. Hiding any detail of the situation is an act of shame that may come from a desire not to change. Discover more about this in 'Thinking for Yourself' – chapter 2 Shame.

Pride and shame are two sides of the same coin.

The definition of pride and shame is all up to you. We are the only ones who can make our decisions, we are responsible for every decision that we make. If we choose to take pride when it is going well then subsequently, we also choose to take shame when it is not going well. I'm sorry to burst any illusions but we don't have that much control. As disappointing as it may seem, we do not and cannot have complete control over our environment. We do not have control over the people around us or complete control over the things around us. The only power we have complete control over (if you choose to accept it), is our own choices.

We are given opportunities, but we make the choice.

As freeing as it is, we do not and cannot have complete control over our environment. We can't create an opportunity in and by ourselves. All we can do is look for the opportunities that already exist and we can make our decisions. The choices we have are to work together; to create an environment where everyone has the opportunity to learn, grow and share. Or to work alone; to protect and save what we have in this moment.

Knowledge will never protect us.

Receiving information without changing will cause increased pain, hurt, and torment. We all receive information through people and communication. It is not the people that can hurt us but the information we receive from them that may cause hurt in us.

Information will come; change will occur.

When we strive to protect our information, we are holding onto a rope while it is cutting our hand. We often hold onto it tighter the more it hurts. The pain and damage to ourselves increase the longer and tighter we hold on.

While we focus on the rope and pain, we don't look for a better option. While we continue to hold onto that expectation because it seems like the safest option, we don't give ourselves the opportunity to step on a ledge and move to higher ground.

Continually taking from other will cause many rope burns.

While we spend our energy holding onto these ropes, we want something from them. We accept the pain as we don't see the ground. We may want to protect these connections because we don't see or understand a better connection.

While we consume our connections, we don't invest in them.

If both ends a connection are pulling against each other, it causes nothing but pain for both parties. While playing tug of war with a partner, we will never 'win' against anyone else. When our adversary is our partner, we fight against the very thing we desire most: connection.

Chapter 4

Connection

Without an understanding of the process, we don't understand our need for connection.

Connection is a basic human need and to deny ourselves this is to deny ourselves our part in the world. When we deny our desire for connection to others, it is easier for them to deny their desire to connect with us.

I believe if we have a void inside of us and we are searching for something to fill it, the answer is connection.

Connection to what, I cannot say. There are different types of connections, but for this part I would like to talk about the human-to-human need for connection. The ability to relate to someone who is fundamentally the same as ourselves and at the same time so intrinsically different.

Connection is easy to find.

Connections are one of the easiest things to find, but sustainable connections are another matter. Maintaining connections that we form seems to be a weakening art. Due to social media and dating profiles, getting a hit to satisfy our instant desire for connection can be easy like a hit of an addiction. Before going out and looking for any easy connection we can find, it is best to decern what kind of connection we actually desire. Surface level connections are not going to satisfy our deep desires for very long. Whatever connection is easiest and quickest to find, is probably a connection you are not going to value very highly. These types of connections typically don't last as they are not valued due to the lack of investment needed to create a hit.

How can I assume that we will not be satisfied by these connections?
If they're easy for us to find, then why are we not satisfied by it?

True, lasting, and trustworthy connection is built through consistency. In relationships we get out of them what we put in. The best way to build a true, lasting, trustworthy connection, is to be true, consistent, and trustworthy.

True connection is built, not found.

Investing in a connection, will strengthen the connection. Valuing a connection will help you to invest in it. The more we value all connections the more sustainable they are and will become. Being consistent with the connection we invest in will mean a strengthening of these connection, leading to a deeper level of connection.

It's a cycle of giving and taking; or sharing.

When we build a connection we give and take, when we move to another connection we give and take. We share who we are, but we also share the experiences we have had in our life and with other people. Whether we do this subconsciously or consciously, we grow through every interaction and connection.

We need connections, not just a connection.

Lasting and consistent connections are not built with one person or with one group. Connections with a singular focus can quickly become dependent. Dependence comes from a need to consume. Connection comes from a need to relate. The asset of seeking connections is that not one person or group will agree with or invest in every part that makes up who one is as a whole. If we only have one friend or one group, it will be easier for us to conform to that person or group. Not conforming to that person or group means that we have no connections. Our need for connection can outweigh our need for our own thoughts and feelings.

More than one connection is needed to satisfy our needs.

If you can picture for a moment, setting up the foundations of a house. This house has pillars supporting it. If this house only has one pillar it would be easy to knock down and the house would fall to the ground. If it had four pillars of different heights and reliability, it may survive if one post was knocked out. The other three pillars could stabilize while the fourth is repaired or replaced. While a number of connections are good, consistent connections are better.

The more post or connection we have as our foundations the more stable the foundation.

When we have inconsistent pillars as the foundation of our house, it leads to cracks and damages due to movement. Having one high pillar and three short pillars may work for a while, but the house will eventually bend if an investment is not made to the other pillars.

Too many pillars and connections lead to a house with no ventilation or breathing space.

Taking from too many connections can lead to undervaluing our connections. We may spend all our time investing, maintaining and building, but not being able to appreciate our connections. Living a life consistently searching for the next connection, or investing time in intentionally growing connections, can inadvertently stop us from just enjoying the connections we have.

A house to rest in.

When spending all our time building and renovating a house, it can be hard to just enjoy and share it. If we haven't yet, it's good to spend some time building and investing in good, consistent, and trustworthy connections. As time goes by, we will lose some and gain some. The strong ones will remain, the cracked ones can be maintained, and the rotting ones can be replaced. With a firm foundation of connections, changes won't shake us or send us crashing to the ground. Changes will just be part of time playing its part. When we do feel a little shift or wobble in our foundations, we can check our connections.

Staying aware of our connections.

When we are aware of the importance our connections have, we recognise when they need a little extra attention or maintenance. Maintaining healthy connections rather than rebuilding new ones after we have given up due to exhaustion, takes less time and energy. We understand and are supported by a deep acceptance from, of and through our connections.

Maintaining our house for the sake of others.

When we are looking at improving and maintaining our own building, we need to keep in mind we already have connections. Where we live is connected to a town, a city, or a country, we too are connected to the places around us, by roads, pathways, waterways, and internet.

When we maintain our house, we can help others stabilize their pillars. We are connected to the people around us.

When we maintain our house or place, we set a standard for our community. Not looking after our place will devalue the places around us. Not valuing the connections we have, will undervalue the connections still to come. When we start investing in and looking after our own place, the places around us can be inspired to do the same. Not by asking or telling, but by the simple observation of the change at our place. Seeing the simple improvements on our place, can create a flow on through our connections. This allows others to be better and it's not that hard.

If a loss of connection happens through this process, we are still able to unite.

Losing a connection indicates that their value of our connection is less than something else. This will allow us to see our choice of holding onto the rope through tough times.

Chapter 5

Understanding Unity

The foundations in which we build our lives determine a number of things.

Just some of them are how we see ourselves, how we see others and how we see the world in general.

When we don't have a good view of ourselves, we can't believe someone else is fully good, when we multiply those views, we don't believe that the world is good. How we see ourselves is what we believe other people are really thinking inside. When we look for evidence it through our connections, we believe that it is how it is for everyone, then everyone must be like us on some level.

The chances are that you are doing the very best you can in life.

Sure, we make mistakes, we get burnt out and maybe what we focus on may not be the best sometimes, but deep down we may want better. We may want to do better, be better and we may want the world to be safer. I know you want better because you are willing to invest in your time in reading this book.

We can unite on so many different levels.

We can unite with what we do, where and how we spend our time. We could walk with people, we could catch a train with people, we could notice the same car in traffic, as we spend time with the same people every day. We connect with them through the acceptance that they exist through the observation of their existence.

We may unite with the way they think, or what we believe. We may have conversations and ask questions. We may have the same passions and desires. We may get curious and discuss a book, or a video or a podcast that we have both heard. We stimulate and expand our knowledge and understanding through these interactions with others.

We can unite in cause, what we view as success or what we dedicate our lives to. This is our underlying reason or our reason why. This is what gives us the energy to do what we need to do. We unite in what gets us emotional and for what we care. One of these can be done by a simple prayer or thought. If there has been people hurt or suffering, we tend to hear about it on the news, but can feel powerless to help them, but we can unite in cause.

Each one of these connections can happen without the others.

We can unite in cause with someone we have never seen and who live on the other side of the world. Like the children starving in another country, the not-for-profit organisation that we donate to, or maybe that person we once knew. We talk to administration worker of companies and organisations. We don't meet them; they just tell us information, or we inform them and that's a chance to unite. Each connection gives us the opportunity to gain experience in another connection. The more connections that we grow, the easier it is to unite.

Unite with our friends.

Chances are we have more connections to our friends then we do with the person we spoke to on the phone about a tech issue. We put more time into those who are easy to build connections with, those who agree with what we do, how we think and what we see to be important. It's so much more than just that.

We have memories with our friends too.

We have shared times, certain points in our relationship where our connection was strengthened. We invested in it because the good far outweighed the bad.

The building of these connections brings greater unity.

The more connections you have the stronger the unity. We also establish connection in the past, present, and future. We connect with those we are raised with because we can see and understand a lot more of who they are because chances are we have experienced similar things. We also plan to do things in the future. Whether we plan to meet for a cuppa, an event or plan a holiday together we form unity through those connections.

We are able to unite.

All of these areas need to have connection. I believe every part of us is connected to the outside world, it's just the strength of the connection that varies.

- We have all had physical touch connection in the past and we will in the future. Right now, we may not be touching someone, but we are touching something. We are present in this world.
- We all have mental connections through conversations, learning and teaching. We have all exchanged information with someone in the past, we will in the

future and right now we are thinking and learning about how we can bring unity.
- We all have a deeper cause, whether we like to admit it or not. We all have feelings and emotions that are not of ourselves and can't be fully understood. Although it may not be obvious right now, when you think about how you are feeling, you are feeling something. We have all experienced feelings and emotions in the past and we will continue to decern our feelings in the future. While we don't feel, we don't live.

All of these points require connection.

Each point I have discussed needs to be connected to others. Notice I said others. All of these points do not and most probably cannot be filled by one person. We need friends, many friends, family, acquaintances and strangers to fill these needs. No one person can fill our needs and we cannot fill one person's needs completely, no matter how hard we try. If we try to be everything to someone else, we will forget that we need to be us, a unique individual.

Each connection needs to be invested in and received in some way.

In the process of taking and sharing unity will grow. When we take and then share, we breath in and out. We don't breathe out everything we breathed in, we keep the interest, the food, the sustenance we need to keep living. With each exchange there is increase, there is another point of view, another experience, another hope that is realised. We don't pass the connection on; we share the connections and bring increase.

Positive connections are like fresh air.

Unity brought about by positive connections will bring freedom, understanding and clarity. Negative connections will bring doubt, shame and confusion. Unity found in the negative will decrease energy. Unity found in positive connections will increase energy.

- A hand-shack is going to feed our requirement for physical connection; a slap will deplete our physical connection.
- A respectful, accepting conversation will grow our requirement for a mental connection; an aggressive and manipulating conversation will diminish it.
- A healthy number of feelings and affection will inspire and encourage us; an intense amount or neglect of feelings will encourage negative growth, locking us in a cycle of looking for the next connection.

It's the connection not the person.

Everyone struggles with at least one area of life. If a connection we have seems to connect to a negative point for one or both parties, we can change the connection. We will never be able to change another person. They are the only person who can make their decisions. What we can do is change the point of connection. We don't need to focus on the negative connection but start building a positive one. Over time we can grow a strong connection with another point and the negative connection will not seem so important. While the pressure is taken off the point or pillar it will be easier to straighten its position. If we are unbale to find a strong connection to another point, it may be time to invest our time and energy elsewhere.

We all crave connection, no matter who we are.

If our connections are bad, we think others are bad. If our connections are good, we think other are good. By investing in the positive connections, we grow and invest in the good of others. We build unity, united in sustainable and enjoyable connections.

If this is true for you, it is true for everyone.

If deep down, at the core of what we need is connection, then everyone will continue to look for it until they find it.
If everyone we know or have ever met is looking for connection, and have not found it, they will continue looking.

Everyone seems to be looking for something.

We may not know what they are looking for, but we know if we are not content. If we are looking for security, it comes through unity. If we are looking for acceptance, it comes through unity. If we are looking for enjoyment, it comes through unity.

Negative things can unite too.

Although this is true, it is not something to worry about. I strongly believe that negative connections will never thrive for a few reasons.

1. Bad actions, bad ideas and bad concepts rise, but they never stay. Most negative connections come from a naivety or misconceptions. All come from self-centeredness and a need to protect ourselves. When our deepest need is to protect ourselves, we can never truly unite. Any group that tries to unite under this idea will destroy each other.
2. Momentum needs people. If no one agrees with what the group stands for, no one will join. People may not understand what unites a group, but eventually people need a reason to return. When negative group intentions are revealed, people will either walk away or not join. Groups or Communities need members and without members they have no momentum.
3. Good people make a difference. There are too many good people in this world to let them win. How many times have you thought something negative would happen and then someone comes to save the day? People may not know what to do for a while, but there comes a point when the negativity grows to a point

that they can no longer walk away, they see no option but to take a stand and encourage positive change.

Only the good will stand the test of time.

When people find a good thing, they share it more easily. This is the test of this series. If you find these things to work for you, if you find them to be true, please share it. If after reading these books you have a greater understanding and sense of freedom, please tell your friends. Not for me, but for them and for the next generations. Pass it on for the people who don't know what they are looking for, but who are unsure what a healthy connection is.

Not just for one life will a change occur.

This book is not about one life that it has changed. Even though there is nothing more important than one life, this change is for the communities. It's for the unity it brings and the amazing things that can happen through people coming together.

This is how I see all things are used for good.

This is all my understanding. I have seen evidence to prove it true but have not seen evidence to prove it false. I'm trusting that through community it will be proven undeniably true.

Unity Summary

We cannot do life alone.

We have all been reliant on other people.

Different people hold different beliefs.

Together everything multiplies.

Good things always advance faster and easier.

Our value comes through our connections.

Connecting with others is a good and wise investments of time.

I know people are good, intelligent and trustworthy.

2

Compassion

Understanding people and having compassion for their feelings.

Chapter 6

Compassionate

Compassion is a unity with someone through a mutual feeling.

It isn't just a deep feeling of sympathy or sorrow for another person or their situation. It is a desire to be connected and understand the persons point of view. When we establish or invest in connections. We connect at a point of similarity. These are not always the same but similar.

Compassion is needed when a connection goes through change.

Being compassionate is needed because we are all different and all unique. Everyone processes change differently, at different times and with different reasons. When change occurs, there is a heightened state of emotions.

There are different types of change.

When someone has a positive change in their life, a compassionate person will celebrate with them. When it is a negative change, they can console, and when they are not sure how they feel about a change, compassion is needed to assist in understanding.
Some people refer to compassion in the negative sense, helping someone through a loss, grief or trauma. Whether positive or negative, every change needs to be processed. Allowing people to process their own feelings through a change, takes understanding and needs patience.

Patience is easier with compassion.

Compassion is not only at a point, or in the moment of change, but throughout a connection. A connection is a continual growth of understanding how the other feels. Understand that compassion and patience go hand-in hand. One is not complete without the other.

Different types of compassion.

Compassion is needed in different ways; short term, long term and deferred/transferred.

Short term is when a person just needs space. Space to evaluate and understand their own feelings. The best thing for this is to remove our own feelings from the situation. Give them the space to experience and understand their own experience. Not putting our ideas or theologies in as they will be unhelpful to the person trying to understand themselves.

Long term happens after short term compassion (space) has taken place and a resolution is not found. Long term compassion is needed when either a major change has taken place, or the person is unable to understand their feelings about the situation.

When a major change happens, deferred or transferred compassion is needed as that one change will bring about subsequent changes.

Major changes are things such as, a physical long-term impairment, a change in a long-term relationship or a death of a loved one. It's more than a quick acceptance of the situation. There are many implications and changes that need to take place after the major one. With every small decision and situation, the person will be experiencing new emotions (emotions not feelings). New thoughts will come up as they change the picture they had for their future. With every change of thought there are feelings to evaluate.

Continue to give space as needed and be willing to make any minor but present decision that they may be overwhelmed with. We can do this by looking after the practical side of those changes. This can allow the person to do only what they can do, that is processing their own feelings. The

key is to remember that this is their change; their loss, their grief or their trauma. We can't start to understand how they are feeling without them telling us. The only way they can tell us, is if they have time to process them.
This is compassion for others. To process or own changes we can couple this with information found in 'Thinking for Yourself'

Compassion can also look like a sounding board.

When people are having trouble understanding their emotions after a change, they may need a sounding board. People who verbally process or ask lots of questions are generally trying to understand what they are missing. It's a way of looking a connection. They know there is a missing link, it's just finding a platform in which to discover it.

Deferred/transferred compassion are term I use to understand this process.

This is when short term and long-term compassion have not been received. Deferred occurs through compassion not being given, and transferred compassion occurs when compassion has not been accepted.

Deferred compassion is always bigger than the original amount needed. When a need is not fulfilled in a timely manner that need will increase over time.

Transferred compassion is when a person doesn't realise their need for compassion and so they can get frustrated with the connections. More about this in Chapter 8.

Compassion is needed when an expectation or assumption is not met with reality.

True, genuine, sustainable compassion is to understand someone else's feelings, purpose and beliefs are different to our own. Giving them space to feel their feelings, while remaining comfortable with our own feelings. When someone else is sad or going through a tough time, it's ok to be happy about unrelated good news that we receive.

Being compassionate is focusing on others and their feelings for a time.

Having compassion is giving space for someone else's feelings for a time to experience and understand that person's feelings. This is how we build a united connection.
We can celebrate with them, and we can sympathies with them. What we can't do is stop them from feeling.

Don't take ownership.

Their feelings are still their feeling. We are unable to take their feeling off them. When we try to do this, all we are doing is multiplying the feeling. This means there is now more to deal with, more to process and this does not help either the helped or the helper.

We multiply what we share.

As in the Unity section, it is through our connections that we multiply everything we share. When we share negative feelings, they multiply. When we share positive feelings they multiply. We only want to share and grow the positive ones. We want to understand the expectation or assumption that caused the negative one so we can choose to process it or change it.

The ancient etiquette of mourning.

In times gone by compassion looked different to today's interpretation. There was a custom around the burial and grieving process of the family. This custom involved support people being available to the grieving relatives. During the grieving process mirrors would be covered, people would abstain from celebratory behaviours. The support people would provide food, clean, and partake in the general running of the house, giving them grieving time and space to be process the change.

The most amazing thing about this custom is that the support person would always accompany the grieving, but they would not speak. They would just be there seeing to it that the grievers are fed and watered, that all their physical needs are being met while they process their own feelings and make decisions that only they can make. The support person was only to speak if they were spoken to. They would be there, present, and available to the person, not trying to find the right words to say or making their presence known, but to serve the grieving and to offer the comfort of their presence.

Being compassionate is a choice.

We choose to invest in the connections we have, we choose to be there for people, we choose to unite. Compassion for other people, doesn't have to wear us out or become a chore. When done in a healthy way it can be both fulfilling, beneficial, and freeing for both parties.

It's only when we assume responsibility for someone else's choices that it becomes exhausting and burdensome.

Compassion is giving people the space to process their feeling and thoughts i.e. emotions.

Being present, serving and speaking when spoken to, builds connection. Sharing of knowledge can help if asked but the most important thing when it comes to compassion is to ensure basic needs are meet. We practice short term compassion on a daily basis, through every interaction we have. We can enjoy the time spent understanding others.

Chapter 7

Unique

I'm sure you know by now I believe that we are all unique.

This is a fact that no one can deny, for by denying it they prove it to be true.

Even though we are all fundamentally the same, we all have a different vision for our lives.

We have an expectation on what will happen in the next hour, week or year. We assume things will be the same as they were yesterday. We may anticipate change, but we can't know for certain what will happen.

Our experiences and what we have been exposed to is different.

Where we lived, who raised us, and what our daily lives look like is all different. These get passed down from generation to generation, multiplying as they go. They also make us all different.

People who are shorter, have children who are shorter. People who are taller, have children who are taller.

It's a general fact of life, but this can also become evident in the way of thinking as well.

Not always is our DNA.

Obesity is not a genetic trait, but it generally runs in families due to the beliefs and habits that are passed down through the connection we have.

I only use this as an example because it is able to be measured. There are many other habits and beliefs that we can pass down to our children, or on to the people around us sub-consciously. Although we may not generally have deep conversations about the way we think about these things, the way we think is evident by the way we act.

People can say many things.

People can spend time convincing us that they believe or act a certain way, but it is their actions that speak louder than words. If we spend enough time around a person who always yells, it will be easy to start yelling also. If we spend time with someone who whispers, we may start whispering back without realising it.

It's all about what we choose to accept as normal.

Normal is what we accept and see on a daily basis. It's not the one-off events or what we do when we have the energy. Normal is how it is the majority of the time. The person who defines the normal in our lives is us. If we choose not to walk away from negative behaviour; if we choose to answer the back chat, if we choose to keep reaching out to those who don't reach back; that becomes the normal.

Everyone has been hurt at one stage or another.

Hurt or pain can also be defined as a change of expectation. Everyone has hoped for something and not had it come true. Does that mean we stop hoping? Logic may tell us that if desiring something we don't have or can't get cause pain, then stopping the desire will stop the pain. But without desires we have no hope; we have no joy, no progress and no success. Without joy we have no driving force; no motivation and we have no energy.

Different expectations.

Two people who experience the same event from the same side can react differently. How we react is a combination of what we have experienced in the past, where we want to go in the future and our current expectation of the unfolding event. It's only through the realisation that people having different expectations is why hurt occurs.

Unmet expectations can ruin a connection.

If we have been hurt or experienced hurt in a certain way in the past, we are more likely to expect to be hurt in the same way again. Depending how we have processed our past experiences, will indicate what we envision now and in the future.

Unvalidated experiences can ruin connections.

If everyone's past is not the same and our future is relative to our past, how many different options and opportunities do we have to be unique individuals. How many different expectations can be had for just one moment in time? It then comes down to the expectation, and the value of the connection compared to the value of the expectation.

Our expectations, experiences and feelings are all different.

Although this is true, it doesn't change the fact that we were all born of women, we all have a body, a mind and spirit. By understanding each other's expectations, experiences and feelings, we understand the things that make us different.

Every person reading this has a past, a present and a future.

We are all searching for some type of connection, although the connection we search for may vary, the search is the same.
We have all been hurt in some way, although the pain may vary, we all ask why.
We were all born for a reason, although our purpose may vary, as we look for it, it will be revealed to each of us.

No two can sustain every connection.

When we look at the money in our wallets, whether they be coins or notes, they will all be slightly different. Even money of the same value, made in the same machine, in the same year, after time they all look different. Though they all were printed and started their journey in the same place, everyone has a different journey from there. Two cions may have stayed together for a time, but eventually they will be separated by a purchase or by a falling away.

The worth doesn't change, but the value varies.

The older the coin gets the more variances are found in them. Coin collecting has been one of my hobbies in times past. Thinking of how many times it has been used to purchase something, wondering the value of its use. A dollar coin is only the value of a dollar at the point of an exchange. While that dollar coin is sitting in our wallet or our safe place, it does not hold the value of a dollar.

The value of the dollar only becomes apparent at the point of exchange.

When the dollar is used to purchase food or supplies, it is only at the point of exchange that it's potential is established. Its value is only determined by how much can be purchased with it. It's worth remains the same. Its value can change due to circumstances, environment and inflation; the amount of food and supplies this dollar can purchase can vary. The same amount of money could be used to buy vegetables or medicine. It could be used to buy a punnet of strawberries or a strawberry plant. Same worth, different value.

The exchange of value.

If we purchase a house, we value the purchase more than the money in our possession. We haggle the price depending on how much we value it. The house is still worth the same, it is a roof over our head, the value comes out in its features.

Someone who values space over convenience will purchase a house out of town. A house with an entertainment area and no garage would be valued more than a house with a garage and no entertaining area for someone who doesn't have a car.

The worth doesn't change but we choose its value according to our beliefs, likes and purpose.

Every connection is still a connection.

The worth of a connection doesn't change, how important it is to us and how we invest in it will determine its value.

When we understand that we can value a connection without changing the person's worth, we understand that by valuing a different connection, we don't change that person's worth.

When we know we are unique, we can value what makes us different.

Fortunately, we are all worthy of life, that's something we can do nothing about. If we weren't, we wouldn't be alive.

How we value life is how others will value us.

Unlike the coins, who have passed through many hands and been part of many exchanges, we have a choice. Coins are dropped, damaged and can be hidden in the bottom of washing machines or couches for years. We have a choice. When we value the choices we have, others will value our choices. When we value our connections and allow them to make their choices, healthy sustainable connections will by established and invested in.

Our expectations don't need to change our ability to be unique.

If we have been let down, our worth doesn't change.
If we've been hurt, we know our worth doesn't change.
If we have been hiding from the world or stuck and can't get out, our worth doesn't change.

If our expectations are not met, it doesn't mean we have to change them to the expectations of our connection.
When we see and value who we are, others will see and learn to value who we are.

Our expectations need to be communicated to our connection.

The value we bring at the point of change, can build or diminish a connection, it is our choice.
It would be unrealistic to define the colour of a person's hair by looking at their hand, or the colour of their eyes by looking at their mouth. In the same way it would be unrealistic to define a persons worth by how similar they are to us or how much we value them.

Are we going to value the opportunity we have to strengthen the connection?
Can we accept the changes we need to make?
Will we communicate our expectations to the other person?

Our value is determined by our beliefs, choices, and trust. Our worth doesn't change.

How much we value other people comes down to our beliefs, our choices and our trust. Their worth doesn't change just because we don't value them.

When I value a person, will they value me?

Noone can guarantee this. If I like a person, it doesn't mean they will like me. When we value the connection we have with people, we add value to both of us.

Interesting big families.

Not just because I wonder how the parents do it, but because every child is different. We can have a family of six children who all grew up in the same house, with the same parents, and if twins, even at the same time. Yet they are all so different. I used to babysit twin girls, identical twin girls. They were lovely and adorable, and could hardly be told apart. Even wearing matching outfits for the first number of years could never change that they are different inside. At that early age I noticed small differences, I found one to be more relaxed and the other more focused. Watching them as they have grown into amazing young women, I see the different places they have been and the different people they are now. Those small differences seen as toddlers, have now multiplied into them finding, creating and living their own purposes, and enjoying their own lives, living very different lives.

Chapter 8

Boundries

Boundaries are needed when the connections we have are not valued.

We all have the same worth and the same opportunities to make our choices. We need to understand that our choices are our choices and people who undervalue our ability to make our own choices, undervalues us. In order for this to be true, we also need to recognize that other people's choices are their choice. Confusion of this nearly always happens due to a lack of understand and always because of a lack of boundaries.

When we know we are all worth the same, we don't feel the need to undervalue the person.

When we know our expectations, experiences and feelings, we can make a choice of what we value. When we have checked our intentions we can then choose to value them over a connection. Remember that we are valuing our intention more than our connection with a person and not the person themselves. If we put them down, we put ourselves down because we are all worth the same. We all make our own choices.

Our value depends on the exchange.

When our worth is not valued, we need to establish our ability to make our own choices. We can continue to be part of a connection when our worth is agreed. The value of our content is defined by the change it brings. If it is not valued the exchange is not complete. Remember that we often have more than one point of connection with one person.

Value each connection to the value given.

Just because we don't see eye to eye on one matter, it doesn't mean that all our connections are now not of any value.

All our decisions are made to move towards connections.

The deciding point is what connection do we seek?

Sitting at a table with an array of food, I may go for the meat first and you go for the salad first. I am not hurt that your preference is different to mine. It serves me well to have different interest, as I can enjoy more of what I enjoy. I am able to learn from you and why you made your decision. I understand more of who you are and your needs, this may help me understand myself better by gaining a new perspective.

My decision is not, right and yours wrong. I don't see mine as being better than yours, just different. If I would like some salad, I am able to have some as well, not to take yours but to share the experience.

Our mutual desire to move towards a connection, is not hindered by our different experiences.

When we spend time with people who appreciate their uniqueness and desire healthy connection, we can appreciate what makes us unique.

Healthy connections are made intentionally.

People who don't value us, don't value the same connection as we do.

If someone is interested in car racing, they may want to be at the track or working on the cars. They are not going to spend much time with a person who doesn't like cars, speed, noise or being outside.

Their love lies in different things. Telling one or the other that they need to change to have a connection is a myth. Their point of connection is just not in cars. They value the connection that they do have more than the one point where they don't connect. When all the car racing, speed, noise and oil doesn't fill their need for connection, they have a choice in what they value more, a feeling or a connection.

When we are exposed to new things and experience new things, we change.

Our hobbies and interest vary throughout our life. As a child we may have wanted to be an astronaut or a Rockstar. As we grew up and, discovered our gifting's and what we enjoyed, we discover our value and our vision changes.

When our vision changes, our connections change.

Within existing connection, we have an expectation of what that connection is giving us. In some relationships, the expectation of each party varies.

My expectation of relationships is that I am supported in my uniqueness and adventures. Why, because my aim is to support others in their uniqueness and adventures.

A relationship between two people who have different expectations of the connection is difficult. It's feeling torn between their purpose and our purpose. It may be difficult because we are trying to maintain a point of connection where our expectations are different. We will both be constantly having to make the choice between that point of connection or our own purposes.

Assumptions come from negative expectations.

When we have an expectation that relationships will just work, we assume they can read our minds. An expectation that their world revolves around us, or more accurately our life revolves around them. Understanding can never come from assuming. Understanding can only come through communication.

Valuing their choices, more than they do.

When we have a connection with someone who struggles to think for themselves, we can show them compassion as laid out in the last chapter. What we can't do, is think for them. We can encourage them to make their own choices, but we can't make that choice for them. We can be there to help them up, but we can't make them take it and we can't change for them.

Trust is built not earnt.

When their expectation of the connection is that we think for them, the connection needs boundaries. The first step is learning how to trust themselves. We may feel drained and pressured after spending time with them. They may expect us to always help them, hold their mindsets or have compassion for them. They may have put an expectation on us to think and choose for them. If they trust us more than they trust themselves it can be tempting to make the choice for them, but this will only enforce this as normal behaviour and not give them the exposure they need to make their own decisions.

The core reasons for this type of connection, is unequal expectations.

When two people have unequal expectations of the connection, we need to explain our expectations. Like in every point of exchange there comes an opportunity to change. One way to change the expectations of the relationship is through communication.

Another way to set boundaries is through changing our own behaviour by changing our own habits. We can change the expectation of a connection by changing our response to it, by changing our response consistently, we change their expectation. We change what they expect by changing what we accept.

All of our experiences and exposures were displayed to us through our connections.

Behavioural traits are learnt through our connections. Changing what we accept will change their behaviour towards us. This will either enhance the connection (they may find you more compassionate, accepting, and trustworthy), or they will make a choice to move away from the connection.

Their choices are their choices.

They may try to change it back to the way it was, the way that worked best for them. They may get angry, frustrated and try ways to change it back to what was easy and worked for them. They may hide or pull away choosing not to value the connection, and the connection slips away.
Whatever they choose to do, let them have their choice, but don't expect things to never change.

How they react and the choices they make are not our responsibility. Our decision lies in what points of connections we value most and whether our expectations are going to change.

All our expectation are received through our previous experiences and exposures.

We can use our previous connections to set up standards that works for both parties. Making these decisions and setting up a standard of behaviour doesn't happen straight away. We have to be patient in this process, we have to understand that it takes time for us and others to understand. We have to let the picture be revealed. We can trust our beliefs and that we are doing the best thing, even when our world seems to be moving and changing so quickly. It is only through the letting go of old connections that we will discover a new and better way.

Continue to believe our worth.

Our life is our life and no one else's. Our purpose is our purpose, and no one can take it from us. Our connections are our connections and only we can know their value and what they produce.

Our value is found at the exchange.

If someone is trying to sell us something, there is an exchange, and we build a connection. When we don't want to buy, there is no exchange, because what they have we don't value enough to make the exchange. By not exchanging what we have, we are able to invest our worth in a connection that will positively impact our value.

Some people may search for their worth in our value.

People who seek the exchange, and not the connection, will need us to change or they will find another to exchange with. They may seek to change us or hope we change them, as they find their worth only by the change.

People may not know their worth or see their value.

People may not want to exchange anything of their own but will try to exchange the worth or value of a third party.

When they believe they have no worth of their own, they will feel they have nothing to add to an exchange and therefore, take the value they have experienced in a previous exchange and pass it on. This is the type of connection will continue to diminish in value.

When someone sees no value in their own opinion, all of their connections may be based around talking about other people, what they did, what they said or what they thought.

Remembering our worth.

Making sure that pride doesn't sneak up in these cases, you are worth as much as the next person, not more, not less. No one is more worthy than another. The value in the connection changes, not the worth of the person. We can continue to show compassion and reveal some beliefs, by showing them the decisions they can make by showing them the decision we are making.

Knowing our own decision.

Always keep in perspective, their worth, and their value. Working towards a community where we all have the connections we need and desire.

To have a different expectation we need to experience a different connection.

When we have only experienced negative expectations within a connection, we only know how to have negative expectations. Setting up new and better expectations will help people experience better connection. Having better connections will encourage bettering our connections.

Whether they choose to stay or go, just know that by showing compassion, we are doing the best thing for them.

It's up to each of us to establish healthy connections. While we accept unhealthy expectation within a connection, the expectation won't change.

Providing a new experience does not have to be complicated.

The change of expectations does not have to end up in a long and deep conversation or a loss of the connection. It happens slowly and consistently in little exchanges.

Save ourselves first.

First, always first, we need to work on our own expectations for our connections. If we don't question our own expectations, we could be taking a healthy connection and putting unhealthy expectations on someone else. Know where our expectations and intentions are coming from.

Do we want to keep it or better it?

Are we displaying our expectations consistently and intentionally?

When establishing a firm expectation of the connection, they find an opportunity.

When we give others the choice whether they would like to stay or leave the connection, we display boundaries. Be prepared that not all connections will survive this process. We will find friends not calling us like they used to, and distance will be created in some connection that we thought would survive.

Before starting this process, we will need to decide whether we would like to invest in other points of connection with this person.

We can value and own our side of the connection, but the bridge needs to be built from both sides.

Between two people is the connection, we can never build their side of the connection. We can't own that part of someone else.

Building a bridge has to happen from each side. We can't create a place for it to land, we have to build our side of the bridge. Each person will help build the bridge from their side until it meets in the middle. Encourage the connection, the interaction and expectation by investing in it. This is where our actions and value matter.

Their worth does not change whether they know it or not.

Their worth remands the same. How much we value the connection is shown by how strong our bridge is. Not how strong the person is, or how good the person is, but how strong the bridge that is our connection.

The relationship is the bridge and not the person.

We have 100% responsibility on the strength of the connection. We have 0% responsibility of who they are and their choices.

We can have compassion for them and give them space to make their own choices, but we cannot make the choice for them. No matter how much it hurts us, or the ones we love.

Connections need vulnerability to build the bridge.

When this vulnerability is mocked or abused, this shows their expectations of the connection is different. There is no harm done. Why? Your worth does not change. Only how much they value you. Move onto a connection that will bring value to both parties.

Not letting someone else undervaluing us or question our worth.

Healthy connections are generally formed slowly and intentionally.

Unhealthy connection can be formed the same way. Connections are formed and enhanced through exchanges where similar beliefs and feelings are encountered.

Connections are hastened during heightened emotional state.

When heightened emotional states occur, we can attach to people who have experienced the same feelings as us. This helps us to process our own feelings and beliefs of the situation because we have found a sounding board in which we can discuss and connect over the similar situation.

I believe they actually have a name for this type of connection. It's a connection that may be good for the short term, but it may also be holding you in a place that belongs in the past. It's a dependent relationship, not a healthy interdependent relationship. What we looking for is an exchange where both parties experience a positive change.

Heightened emotional state can happen for a number of reasons.

Events such as sharing a moment of delight, learning the same lesson, trauma and sex can form an emotional bond.

The most willing type of emotional heightened connection is found through dating apps and sites where the sole purpose is to be in a relationship.

Entering with a sub-conscious agreement.

When we enter into an agreement to experience a heightened emotional state with another person, we share the belief that this is a good thing, a good feeling and that it's filling our need. We receive a moment of relaxation and a feeling of vulnerability, yet walk away without filling the lasting need for a connection.

A connection is formed through every heightened emotional state.

Unhealthy and healthy connections are formed through heightened emotional state. When we invest in, recognise and appreciate the healthy connections we have, we form a new habit. When our desires are met in a healthy and sustainable way, our desire for unhealthy connections will not burden us. We may clearly see our choice of fulfilling as a quick fix that will establish a bad connection, or patiently waiting for a healthy connection that will value both people.

Observe our expectation and gain experience.

Knowing the difference between healthy and unhealthy connections will help us to continue to invest and value healthy connections. We won't miss the unhealthy connections as they fade away as our time will be spent enjoying our healthy connections.

We can be a sounding board but not a punching bag.

We can exercise compassion by assisting and building a positive connection. If we can recognise when unhealthy expectations enter the relationship, we understand that we still have a choice to be in the relationship. The best choice we can make is to communicate our expectations and remove assumptions from the relationship.

Chapter 9

Communication

Communication is the glue that holds people together.

Compassion and connection are only able to happen through communication. Without communication we are not able to relate to others. How we relate to others can happen in a number on ways.

Whether it be verbal, physical or spiritual, we all communicate with each other on these three levels.

Verbal includes spoken, written, typed, and recorded; anything that uses words to articulate thoughts.

Physical, is anything related to our body; hand gestures, crossed legs, crossed arms, frown, smile, slumped body or good posture.

Spiritual communication is a less obvious way of communicating; however, we all give it and receive it. Spiritual communication can come out in our attitude, the way the words are spoken, the emphasis we put on curtain words. It's the difference between written words and spoken words. It's the performance or theatre that comes out through the words.

If you feel you have never experienced this type of communication, I would like to explain a little more.

You walk into a room; the room feels heavy. Everything is in its place, nothing has moved. There could be people in the room, or it could be empty, but there is caution in the air. Nothing looks threatening, but it gives you the creeps. As you move around you notice that the tension is so thick you can cut it with a knife.

This is spiritual communication.

It's not something many people acknowledge or talk about because it is hard to articulate and often goes unnoticed. It is used for drama and romance to create a certain sensation or to reveal intentions.

This is the main way that animals communicate.

Dogs smell fear because we are telling them there is something to be fearful of.

A horse can know whether we have a rope behind our back because of it.

Birds will flock to areas where there is healthy spiritual communication.

This is how I became aware of spiritual communication.

I haven't often spoken about this but since its discovery, it has made a profound change in my life. My discovery was just after my separation. I was going through a hard time and was weeding my garden for some thought processing time. My dog at the time was in her pen. She could not hear or see me but started whimpering. It was a discernibly sad whimper that caused me to investigate. My usually excited dog sat quietly while I opened the gate. She would often go chase hares in the paddock, or bugs in the courts in her eagerness to be out, but today she was quiet.

I let her out and went back to weeding, she sat behind me and followed me along. There was one thought that kept coming to me. It wasn't a good thought, and I honestly don't remember what it was, but every time that thought popped into my head, she would touch me. The first time her paw touched my back I nearly jumped out of my skin. Every time that thought arrived, she would nudge me or put her head on me. Her presence made me realise what that thought was giving me. For a couple of days, she stuck by me fairly close. I became so aware of the thought; I was able to throw it away relatively quickly. A month later I was feeling much better and she was back to her normal energetic self.

It's a communication of the spirit.

Those of us who have a dog as a companion, may know what I am talking about. Unfortunately, spiritual connection with a beloved pet or animal, will not satisfy other needs for long term connection as it can't be developed in other areas. A spiritual connection will grow and improve a connection that has already been established with intellectual and physical connections.

Is there another way we can explain the 'chemistry' that we feel or see between people?

Within each type of communication, there can be a positive and negative connection.

This explains the feeling we receive around some people. Like that person, we just can't trust or that animal that no one can tame. This is the easiest type of communication to project onto others. It comes back to believing that everyone is just like us, meaning our most sub-conscious intentions. Being aware of our deepest reasons or intentions will help to identify if the spirit is coming from us or others.

By being intentional with our communication, we will be intentional with our connections.

Important in maintaining and growing our connections is being aware of what we are putting out, that is what we are giving to others. If we do want connections, yet struggle to obtain or maintain it, it may be because our spiritual communication is working against our physical and verbal communication. Our sub-conscious mind is working against our conscious thoughts.

Physical communication is more than body language.

While having restrictions placed on our physical distance from others, it's important to remember that we do need to communicate with others on a physical level. No comprehensive connection can be made without a physical element. Complete trust cannot grow without acknowledging their presents, then touch and after that affection. Relationships can be sustained through verbal and spiritual process, but relationships can't be deepened without the presence of physical attendants.

Physical connection between people.

We know trust is built through physical presents because in years past the handshake was such an important part of affirming trust. Its incredible importance is confirmed during times of illiteracy. The handshake was as good as, or better by some standards, than a contract. It was a personal promise and a giving of the word, firmly planted in a foundation of trust and integrity. Studies have shown that a child without physical touch will not thrive or grow at the same rate as a child who receives physical touch. It may be the case that children who don't receive physical touch will die from neglect.

Gaining evidence.

The level of touch that people are willing to accept from a person, indicates the level of trust they have for them. This level of trust is also in relation to the level of trust that they have for the other people around them.

Think back to when we first met a particular person.

How much has our trust in them grown or diminished since that time?
Through what communication or interactions did it grow; either negatively or positively?
Is this a common result in the way that we communicate?
What of their traits lead us to either trust them more or less?
Do we possess these traits?

These are important traits to recognised as they can serve as indicators for the level of trust one has in ourselves.

Physical types of communication.

A gentle touch of a friend, a firm handshake, a pat on the back or a cuddle from a person we trust, can work wonders in building our connection and trust in that connection.

In the same way, a slap, a push or a rejected advance of physical affection can diminish the trust within a connection.

Our intellectual communication happens within words.

There is an intellectual transaction however we communicate. For example, you reading this book is an intellectual communication between us. The conversations we've had, the social media posts we interacted with, the messages we respond to, or the book we read, all help build an intellectual connection.

Valuing the intellectual communication we receive and being aware of where it is coming from will help us to become aware of the connections we're establishing.

Communication is not a one-way connection.

As much as we need to be aware of what we are saying on these three levels, we also need to be aware of what others are saying to us on these three levels.

Someone's spirit changes towards us.

When this happens, we can often pick it up, whether we like to admit it or not. We can know if someone suddenly doesn't like us or doesn't have time for us any-more. Confronting and dealing with this is often very hard because it takes a lot of trust in ourselves and what we are interpreting.

If a door is slammed or a snarly face greets us, it is easier to assume that there is tension. If we are unable to put our finger on it, if something just seems different it's harder to know where to go to from there.

It's important to remember the value of the connection, lies in the value we place on each point of our connections.

If we have a connection that we value and notice a change in the connection, we generally have two main options. We can ignore it and not talk about it or address it. Ignoring it will result in the connection moving in a negative direction and may result in a loss of the other connection points that we value. This may eventually turn into a need for control by either us or them if not negotiated through communication.

If we sense a shift in the connection, and we value the connection, then we may raise our concerns. The result could be-
-The connection is fine.

-They are having issues with something else that we may be able to talk through with them.

-There is nothing wrong at all, it may be a shift in our own spirit.

Or

-There is an issue with the connection.

-They didn't know how to raise it with us but would like to resolve it.

-They don't want to talk about it. This could be because they don't feel comfortable and may need time, or they don't value the connection enough to endure a hard conversation.

Either way it is their choice. We are responsible for our part in the connection, not the person.

Listen and value the connection.

When we do this, we want to understand so that we can reach a new depth of connection. If the person chooses not to value our connection, it is their choice. It's not time to walk away but to have compassion for them.

Healthy communication indicates a healthy person.

A healthy person can establish positive connections although we may not be responsible for all of our connections, we are responsible for all of our communication. No one can make us mad or make us do anything. We always have a choice, and so do they. In our connections we may need to help others see their choices in a way that will help them value their connections.

We need to listen more than we speak.

When one person speaks, more than one person can listen. The most important part of communication is the listening. The most important part of listening is understanding. The most important part of understanding is learning. Not everyone reaches a point of giving at the same time. I believe we all have something to give others, but first we need to understand what is needed. Understanding the people around us comes from listening, it comes from absorbing and taking things in. It is only through receiving that we can give.

It's better to take in than to spit out.

One negative word has the same ability to hurt someone as one slap or abrupt push. The difference is negative physical communication is much easier to see and recognise than negative intellectual communication.

Negative intellectual communication can be repeated by the victim if it is not recognised as negative communication. We are all lead by the example of others, a baby learns from their parents. The negative communication that we exercise, can be carried on by others who trust us. They do this not knowing that it may be harmful.

Negative words have far greater power than a negative touch.

The consequences of negative intellectual connection may seem far less important because they are easier to hide. This doesn't change that they are just as damaging if not more damaging because of their ability to remain unchecked. This communication is the easiest way for a healthy connection to turn into an unhealthy one.

We need to find our own interpretation of what works for us and our communication within our connections. Although we are all fundamentally the same, we are all intrinsically different and because of this every connection we have is different. This needs to be discovered and developed within each connection we have. That being said, there are some deciding factors.

The deciding factors are words, actions and spirit.

We may have had someone say sorry to us and then repeatedly do it anyway while believing that their words are sufficient compensation for their actions.

We may have had someone change their actions, but not communicate they are sorry and so we are unsure where we stand and if we can trust them to understand us.

We may have someone who doesn't seem aware that they hurt us. They continue to act the same way, expect the same things and carry on as if nothing has happened.

This is why communicating our forgiveness on all three levels is so important.

When we forgive ourselves for the actions or words we have created, we release the need to hide them. This allows us to be honest and learn why we thought they were our best option and what our intention actually caused us to create. By doing this we build trust in our ability to connect.

Forgiveness of ourselves is not and cannot be dependent on the forgiveness of others.

I know I hurt someone. I know it was unintentionally and I can come up with a million things I did to break that connection. That doesn't change the fact that now I know better, and I am sorry.

'Sorry' is never the first step.

My decision to forgive myself was expressed through a change of words, actions and spirit. I forgave myself for the selfish way of thinking. I thought about how it would look if I was more considerate and changed my actions. I then let them know that I was aware my behaviour was not appreciated. I communicated what I had stopped doing and what I wanted to start. I then gave them the opportunity and means to respond.

Their decision is still their decision.

The only thing I can do is ask for understanding. When they choose to accept my apology and value our connection, the conversations of understanding can again start. Once the conversation of understanding starts, the bridge can start to be rebuilt.

I am not responsible for the person; I am responsible for the connection.

I can only rebuild my end of the bridge; I cannot make a place for it to land.

When we ask how to rebuild the connection, we are saying that we value that connection.
When we change our actions, we are letting them know that we understand their need.
When we apologise for what we created, we are letting the other person know that we want a better connection for both of us and we will now change our ways.

Communicate an apology in three ways.

If an apology is not communicated the expectation of the previous interaction will remain. If the same situation occurs, they will expect us to react in the same way. When we don't admit we can do better, others assume we will stay the same. They assume we value our need to stay the same more than the connection they provide.

Remember we can only make decisions for ourselves.

When understanding is reached and a solution is put forward, we still have a choice- do we value the connection more than the action they are asking us to change?

Bargaining for forgiveness is not true, lasting forgiveness.

Although all connections come with conditions, conditional forgiveness won't last. These conditions may be put forward by both parties on a sub-conscious level. These are spoken about in the chapter 'Boundaries'. We can become aware of these conditions by listening to their communication. People will soon let us know if we are meeting their standard and we do the same.

We can't assume they know what we are thinking.

Assuming they know we are sorry, or assuming that they know what we want, is not valuing the connection. The value of the connection is expressed by the time and effort put into the communication. Remember that a healthy spiritual connection works in cooperation with intellectual and physical connections.

Saying "I'm sorry" is not even half the job done.

If we have a connection that has been negatively affected through our words and actions, and we want to positively effect this connection, consider the following.

After each apology, the connection has an opportunity to grow.

When forgiveness within the connection is reached, we have both made another decision to value this connection. When each of us express that this connection means more to me than; that moment, that problem or another connection we continue to grow in trust. When trust continues to grow the connection continues to grow in a positive way.

Affirm the connection.

If we break the trust and can listen to the words, actions and spirit of the other person, we need to affirm. When trust is broken, then we can rebuild that connection.

Assumptions kill communication.

Assuming we know the other person perfectly, or we know what we did to hurt them is not having compassion and will therefore lead to impatience.

Being patient means valuing the connection more than the time it takes to 'fix' the connection. If we are just looking to constantly fix our connections, we may not be appreciating that points of connection in our lives. Connections, like everything, do not stay still. They are constantly moving and changing. This is why it is important to grow connections, it benefits our trust in people and ourselves.

Each time we trust ourselves a little more, we see there is a little more we can change to trust ourselves more.

Take the people in our lives that we do trust the most. How much access do we give them to our lives?

Again, remember that the person that we need to trust the most is ourselves. Not that we are more important than others, but that we are confident in the value we bring to others. The only one who can discover this value is ourselves.

Try communicating on these three levels.

Developing our awareness of the positive or negative spirit we carry helps us to discern our value. When we discern our value we decide whether we want to connect with another person.

Chapter 10

Understanding Compassion

Understanding people have their own solutions.

Empowering people to find their own solution creates a non-dependent and freeing relationship. I adopted this idea while people presented their "problem" for me to solve. I didn't offer my own thoughts or advice but to be there so they could focus on grieving, processing and establishing a new way of life. The last thing someone who is angry, depressed, or fearful needs is to feel like they have the right to stay there. I am not saying they shouldn't feel a certain way, but life will never progress in a positive way while they want to stay in a negative place.

Our negative feelings encourage a point of change.

While we don't want to change our thoughts or actions, the negative feeling will stay. Being able to reach a point of 'neutral' emotions through our feelings, means that we first need to know where our thoughts are coming from. We need to understand what emotions are and where they are coming from. (There is more on this in "Thinking for yourself"- Thoughts) I want to make clear that we cannot and should not try to put down or hide from feelings. I am referring to emotions, which is the thought or label associated with a feeling. When we can understand where emotions came from, we can pick them up and put them down as needed. This allows us to be totally present in each moment.

My aim is to be flexible in my foundation.

My foundation is a foundation of core beliefs. They are hard to change but above that anything goes. That is anything that fits comfortably on my firm foundation I am willing to try.

Understanding our own feelings will deepen the amount of compassion we have for others.

Understanding our emotions about where our feelings are coming from will help us to build connection and compassion for others. Keeping in mind that everyone has a past, present and future.

Shame verse compassion.

When we have shame about how we feel we are unable to truly experience and evaluate that feeling. By not having compassion we are not accepting the feelings that someone else is feeling. We can in turn shame who they are on a base level. When someone has a feeling that makes us feel uncomfortable, it may be because we are not comfortable having that feeling in us. When we acknowledge and unhealthily encourage a feeling in someone else, we may be trying to justify that feeling within us.

With compassion we have a great opportunity to share humility.

Humility is accepting that no one knows it all. If we expect one person to know and apply everything perfectly to their life, then deep down we would have that same expectation of ourselves. If we expect ourselves to be perfect; by knowing, saying and doing all things right, all the time, that doesn't give us any freedom to learn. When we expect someone else to know, say or do exactly as we do, it does not give them space or freedom to ask, seek and find what they need to do.

Assuming there is only one 'right' way brings pride.

When we have pride in our own way of life and view it as 'right' and all other ways of life as 'wrong', we carry with us the burden of trying to tell everyone to live the way that we are living.

Assuming there is a 'wrong' way.

Assuming everyone else is wrong will not give us an opportunity to learn and understand other people's view of the world. Taking a step back from our own lives and looking with fresh eyes will help us understand that if everyone did what we did there would be no need for us, there would be no need for more than one person. If everyone knew, said and did the same things, no one would miss another of us. There would not be enough space for us to live our lives. We would be a community of machines, not able to think for ourselves. Not everyone can be the same.

Fear only comes from the unknown.

We can want everyone to be the same, so they are predictable. We can want everyone else to be like us because we understand ourselves more than anyone else. When we doubt things are good, fear is the recurrence. When we give ourselves the ability to grow, learn and experience something different, the unknown no longer needs to be feared.

Fear comes from a lack of understanding.

When we choose to stay in the fear, we choose not to understand where it comes from. Understanding our beliefs helps to identify where our fear is rooted. When understanding of the source is reached, we can then process the belief and observe it's effect.

Acknowledging the negative feelings, means we are then empowered to change it.

Understanding that the negative feeling has occurred because something is not the best it can be, gives us a chance to look for something better. Seeing that we can do something better is the only way that we will do it better. Only when we can learn from the choices we have made, can we endeavour to discover a different way and make better choices.

Forgiving ourselves and in turn forgiving others will help us to discover new choices.

Each mindset needs its own foundation on which to build.

In each mindset we have a point that needs to be filled to create a firm foundation in that mindset. When we acknowledge each feeling we can then strengthen that point by strengthening the connection it has with the others.

Fear needs vision and understand emotions.

Shame needs understanding and trust emotions.

Pride needs trust and vision.

When one mindset is weaker than the others, it needs space and time for it to grow. We can help give ourselves the time and space needed to process, grow and strengthen by asking a friend to temporarily hold the other mindsets for us.

This is the process, but it only works when everyone understands and makes their own choices.

When we no longer want to be fearful.
We can ask if we know what we are afraid of. This discovers what thought is attached to the feeling. Moving forward we discover what the future would look like without this thought. We can than ask who we would like to be in the future. Very important to create a vision for both, a negative of the old thought and positive vision of the future. A completely new vision, not a negative of the negative but one that does not relate to the negative. As we are reminded of the vision, we are able to process the forgiveness of the past. This will help us to work out what we are fearful of and how or why we need to forgive.

When we no longer want to feel shame.

We can ask what we feel now and whether we would like or enjoy this feeling. We can ask if we know what we are hiding and what we could learn by revealing it. This will help us discover what the thought is that we are concealing. We can ask what we know to be true, and what we can trust. What things have we learnt in the past and how has that lesson effected our interactions. Our shame more than likely comes from some sort of doubt, a conflicting of our truth and the truth. As these points are held, we can create a new destination or vision for our lives that we can start to work towards. This will be our new direction and the new place we want to be.

And Pride, hmmm.

I feel like pride is the one that we try to deal with on our own. When someone has pride and they don't have anyone they can trust, and it is hard to see the results, so we struggle to recognise it. We don't trust ourselves and often despise our emotions and so struggle to ask for help. The only thing I can suggest and what made a huge difference in my life was having someone to trust. Someone who kept showing up, they didn't do much except be there and be available. People with pride don't like change, and we want things to stay the same. We don't like the unknown and the unpredictable. The only issue with this is that change, the unknown and the unpredictable are the only things guaranteed by life.

When we are told pride is a good thing and that pride helps us, we only end up with division. When we are told that everyone needs pride and we shouldn't change, this is when we fight the most. We fight the outside because we struggle with the fight within.

Pride needs someone to trust.

We need someone who will be there for us, someone we can trust, if we don't have that, we can be that for someone else. We also need to know that not all changes are bad, because it is only by changing that we find a better way. Accepting change means we are able to change again; we are able to continually grow and be better. We learn that although the change may be difficult to accommodate, good things can come on the other side. If we don't have anyone we can trust, we can trust someone. It's our choice to keep hurting or accept the change. Pride needs a positive vision of the future, it's a growing vision. It doesn't always have to be this hard. Where we are right now is not the best things will be, they can get better, but we have to want to go there. Letting go of our own expectations is the only way we can get there.

Everyone's past is made up of good times and bad times.

People have helped us, and people have hurt us. When we focus on the hurt, we tend to think we have to do it on our own. When we don't acknowledge and thank people for the help we have received, we start to think all the good things, came from us alone.

This can lead to a sub-conscious equation-

People = bad, hurt and unreliable.

Me, myself & I = safe, reliable and good.

This, to me is pride. Whether we view pride as an asset or not, we can't have compassion and pride. They can't coexist within one thought. So, the choice is compassion or pride, not both.

If we recognize these traits in someone, are we going to choose compassion or pride?

We can't have patience and pride.

If patience needs compassion and compassion and pride cannot coexist, neither can patience and pride. If we really want patience we need to be accepting of change. We also need to be accepting of others changing through compassion.

Fear, Doubt and Pride.

When someone is wanting to let go of one of these traits, all we can do is show up. We can't tell them what to think, we can't make the decision for them, we can't answer the questions for them, or be their missing piece. All we can do is give them space, and short-term compassion by holding their other mindsets, so they can focus on building the weaker one stronger.

This is something that I have seen work in myself and in other people. By testing it and seeing if it is good, we can learn from our own experiences and exposures. Through a trusting relationship we can build on these foundations.

Compassion Summary

Each one of us is unique, so every connection we have is unique.

Understanding feelings doesn't mean we have to take them on as our own.

Communication is needed for understanding other people.

Understanding is needed to help people discover what we need.

Hiding our feelings can cause others to hide theirs.

Making decisions for someone else diminishes their trust.

Trying to take responsibility for someone else's feelings is not understanding them.

I understand people and have compassion for their feelings.

3

Perseverance

Consistently keeping my priorities in perspective.

Chapter 11

Persevere

Perseverance is consistent action of one's purpose or state.

To be able to be consistent, we have to be confident in our purpose or the state we are pursuing.

We persevere when we go on doing something even though it is difficult.

When we don't have the opportunity in front of us, we trust it will come. When we have the desire for something we don't have the opportunity to obtain, we need to persevere. If our desire aligns with our long-term purpose and goals, then we continue to look for opportunities.

Life is to keep going, to persevere.

When we have the opportunity to get out of bed but not the desire, we need perseverance. When we have the opportunity to move towards our ambition, but not the want, we need to perseverance.

Is giving up an option?

If you ask me, it's not. We only have one life, if we choose to live it, it can be our greatest joy. If we choose to protect it, it can be our biggest burden. If we choose to give it away, we will never have the opportunity to experience a better life than we have right now.

Living life for ourselves.

Life is hard when we live life for ourselves. Our life is easier when our reason for living, exists outside of ourselves. Therefore, our reason for living needs to be so clear. In the hard moments, (there will be moments) when it all seems too hard, we need a clear, definition of 'why' to keep us moving in the best direction.

When we persevere with the opportunities we are given, we continue to discover our desires and purpose.

We are given so many opportunities. When we can clearly say no to the one's we don't want, we become available for the opportunities that we do. If nothing else through the process of elimination, a better opportunity will come. There will come a point when both our desires and purpose will prevail. We will experience a joy that happens when our life's passion and the opportunities we are given align.

Joy will come when we discover the missing piece.

When the opportunities we are given line up with our life's passion, we can then make our choice to exercise our purpose. When we are given a decision, it is important that we make it in line with our priorities. When our priorities consider and are in align with all things that have gone before, we will be given the opportunity. When we persevere with these priorities, they will be realised.

Decisions are easier to make when we look at the other side.

All decisions have two sides. Knowing what is on the other side of the coin will help us to know what our decision is giving us.

Getting out of bed, will get us to work on time. Sleeping in will cause stress, anxiety and may result in being unorganised for the rest of the day.

To persevere is to make decisions.

In the last chapter I wrote about the choice we need to make between the connection and communicating or unhealthy connection and no communication. Valuing the communication will strengthen the connection. Undervaluing or valuing something else more than the communication will create fractures in the connection bridge.

The easy way isn't always going to be the easiest way.

When we want to take the easy way of not communicating, not making decisions, and not dealing with the opportunities we have been given, they will stop being given to us. It may be the easy way in the moment, but it will never get easier. Doing the difficult things when they come, means life gets easier.

The conversation may seem hard, but the consequences will be harder.

Having to establish new connections is harder than maintaining the healthy ones that we already have.

Can we ever run out of connections?

"It's like being around anyone is draining, it's easier to keep to myself."

The more out of practice we are with relationships the harder it is to start and maintain them.

"It's not really that I want to stay home all the time, it's just so exhausting to go out and be around people."

They are still there, if we want connection, if we want friends; we have to have the conversation.

No circumstance or situation will change the way that I behave, or the knowledge that I am accepted.

This is similar to my personal affirmations. It helps me to keep working towards my purpose and priorities. I don't let other people's choices define my purpose. I don't let other people opinions change my identity. I don't let my past mistakes, bad decisions or lack of knowledge define my future.

My daughter hated mandarins.

We were at our favourite farmers markets, buying our fruit and veggies. My children choose their own fruit for the week, sometimes it's something new, and sometimes it's the old favourites. We came across a new stall holder with citrus fruit. My daughter who hates any form of citrus, stood back as the other children made their choice. There was some fruit they hadn't tried before. As they were asking about it, the store owner offered them a taste. They had a piece and passed it on. They loved it and we discovered Pomelo.

The store holder noticed one daughter didn't have a taste. She informed him that she doesn't like them. He asked if there was anything she would like to try, but she declined. We went about our purchase and were ready to leave, when my daughter asked if she could try a mandarin. The store owner obliged. She had a small taste, quickly pulled a sour face and handed it to me. I took it and we moved on. After a moment, she asked for it back, saying 'Actually it's not too bad". She proceeded to eat that piece and another. We purchased mandarins for her fruit, she now enjoys them.

This had me curious, why for over ten years had she believed that mandarins where not good. I will never know the answer but when she was younger, we lived in a town where we were not allowed to have citrus. She didn't know what any citrus was. While on holidays she had tried some citrus that wasn't very nice. My daughter's only experience with mandarins, were that they were not nice, because of this experience she was hesitant to try them again.

Sometimes our past experiences can give us distorted expectations of the future.

Create a vision for a new future. Not relative to your past but to the people around you. Move forward in the direction you would like to go, instead of running from the past you no longer want.

Chapter 12

Ambition

Ambition: a desire to have a life that achieved something.

Ambition is the driving force for patience.

Patience is not sitting and waiting for something to fall in our lap. Patience is about what we do while we are preparing for an opportunity to arrive.

If we have spent our lives waiting, what are we waiting for?

Are we waiting for something different? We could be waiting for an answer, waiting for a partner, waiting for a baby, waiting for our children to grow up, waiting for 'that' job, waiting for a promotion, waiting for that car or that house, waiting for the end of time or waiting for our lives to finish.

We are what we are.

When we are waiting, we are waiting to be enough; good enough, brave enough, smart enough, loving enough, or unique enough, then we will be happy. We are waiting for our lives to count for something.

Our lives do count for something.

We cannot help it; it is something we have no control over. We can't choose not to have a choice or make a decision. We have one.
We can't choose not to have a purpose or spend our time doing something. We do something.
The question is what are we going to do with the time we are given, with our life, our decisions and with our purpose. what are we going to achieve?

When we choose to live in our purpose, we have lasting ambition.

When we choose to hide from our purpose, we are hiding from ourselves. When we choose to protect our life, we don't find our purpose. I've tried hiding and it doesn't work. We end up sad and depressed, we don't see the point in conversations and connection. It's easier in the moment to build up walls and stay inside. It's easier in the moment to invest in loneliness, but the easiest choice now gets hard later; the best choice now gets better.

Ambition takes energy.

To achieve anything takes energy, but it's only though positive achievement that we receive energy. Ask any marketing guru, school or organisation; 'gold stars' work. Recognition for our work gives us energy to keep going. When we take away awards and recognition, the motivation diminishes. When the recognition comes through our connections it establishes a deep trust in the shared intention.

Our ambition is the thing that we desire to do or be.

It may be unclear, there may be things in the way, or we may not even think we are able to achieve it but it's not about having the opportunity now, it's about preparing for the opportunity. We may think we don't have enough time, enough energy or enough intellect, but if we want it enough, we will be enough, do enough and have enough to see it achieved.

Where there's the will, there's a way.

If we believe in something enough to see it through the rough times, we are guaranteed to succeed. We don't know how long, how wide or how deep those rough times will be, but if it is good for ourselves and everyone around us, then we won't be alone in our purpose, the process and the achievement.

Rome wasn't built in a day, and they are still building it.

One of the oldest cities in the world, is still being added to. They are still building, renovating, and restoring buildings. While people are living and working in Rome, there will always be time to have an effect. There will be things to do, buildings to maintain and new ideas to consider. Imagine if they had just waited for it to be finished before living in it and enjoying it.

We are not complete, perfect, or finished, and we won't be until we stop living.

Just like Rome, we will never be perfectly complete and without the need to change. We grow in a positive direction when we know the direction we are growing. Our ambition is to get better, to improve and to have a positive effect on the world.

With every breath we breath, we grow.

Every breath in or out, has the potential to utter words that could change someone's life. That life is our own and it could be someone else's as well. Every breath in, we can take in good or bad, and every breath out, we can create good or bad. We choose to see the positive or negative and we choose to spread the positive or the negative.

Making it positive.

Our choice and what we choose to do with each breath, is so powerful. Do we want to grow the positive and make it easier for ourselves and others? Do we want to grow the negative feelings that are in the world and make it harder on ourselves and others?

If we think of the best person we know, why do we think they are so great?

I can guarantee it is because we value what they have achieved. It will be because of something they have said or done. It will be something that makes them different than others.

Each one of us are also here for a reason.

You can also achieve your purpose for your life. We can be different. We can say, do or be someone different to who we are right now. We can do what we have always wanted to do. We can have those connections we always wanted to have. We can make that difference we've always wanted to make.

Oh, But................(please fill in excuse here)...................

It wasn't easy for the other person either.

Deep down we all have the same enemies. We all fight the same battles, and we all want to live our life.

It doesn't always take courage to take the first step.
Wait, read that again.
It doesn't always take courage to take the first step.

It takes knowledge and understanding.

Knowledge that we have a choice and understand what that choice is giving us. It takes knowing who we are and understanding that we cannot hide who we are and still have the energy to live it. While we keep making that easy choice our life will get harder. That with that hard choice, that one we know is good for everyone and is deep down what we really desire, with that choice, our life will get easier. Making the same choices we have always made, will not allow us to go any further than we have already come.

If we want to grow in life, choose it.

If we want to achieve something in life, then keep choosing it. When we don't, we are choosing anxiety, depression and heart break.

We play a part in this world that no one else can.

Oneself and only ourselves can know our truest desires, so we and only us can achieve those desires. If we want to achieve something we will achieve that thing we have been putting off. That thing we have been running away from. No one else will do it like we can.

Ambition is one of the most powerful energy sources we can have.

Without ambition, we have no energy. We have no sense of self. We have no drive, no passion and no desire. With our unique ambition, we have purpose, and desires, and we recognise the opportunities. We have energy to make those decisions and move on to our next goal.

Perpetual motion.

When we don't invest our energy into achieving our goals, we don't achieve them. When we don't achieve our goals, we find it hard to find the energy to complete our goals. When we invest the energy we have, into achieving our goals, we achieve our goals sooner and by doing so, we gain more energy. Just like perpetual motion, it can be hard to start the wheel turning, but once it is started, it is easier to keep the wheel turning than it is to stop it.

Holding onto an ambition that is slowing us down.

If the perpetual motion is hard to continue it may be because it comes from an unreliable or internal source of energy. Our focus may not be our true ambition. A sustainable ambition is one that is for the good of everyone. It gives achievements to our lives and to the lives of others.

What is the energy that is holding us back?

Is there something that would positively add to the people around us? If we want to invest our energy somewhere, invest it in others. Don't let a bad tasting mandarin, keep us from enjoying the opportunities we are given.

We have more than a little energy.

I know all of this may seem like hard work, but when we look at the other side of the coin we can understand more. Do we want to choose something that diminishes our energy, leading to sadness and depression? Do we want to choose that which will continue to take our energy and not give anything in return?

What is the worst that could happen?

If we try something new and it's not for us, we can learn and try again. We don't see it as a waste of time but learning what we didn't know.

We are finding our own purpose and not taking someone else's. This takes time. Our purpose cannot be replaced, just like the purpose of others cannot be replaced.

We have the qualities needed for the opportunities we are given.

We can't take someone else's purpose. Don't be a giraffe trying to win a dolphin race. Be a giraffe, easily reaching those things that others struggle to see. Be content letting the dolphins swim the sea. A dolphin trying to eat the leaves from a tree will struggle harder and when they have achieved their 'purpose', they will not appreciate the reward as the leaves will taste bitter in their mouth.

Chancing chess.

Just like the game of chess, we cannot win if we don't take the chance of losing a few pieces. We will lose the game if our main focus is to protect our king. Losing pieces doesn't mean losing the game.

Taking time to forgive ourselves is not losing the game, it is the process of wining. There is no shame, just learning. The worst thing we can hurt is our pride.

Achieving a goal will inspire us to set and achieve another.

Having an ambition to work towards will give us energy. When we keep our purpose at the front of our minds, we can't help but see the opportunities to walk in it.

We will start to serve people, not so we are good enough, but because we are good enough; not so we can be different, but because we are different.

Serving from an overflow.

This means that when we can establish healthy thoughts and connections, we can help others. Helping others is not a subtraction of ourselves, but an adding to. Our driving force or energy source becomes generosity rather than protection. Every time we help someone, we want to help someone else. We are not helping for the reward or the accolades, but because we see the positive effect our presence has on people. We are choosing to invest in working together and multiplication of the positive. We notice that doing things for ourselves is needed but being able to do things for others is success.

Success is not measured by what we have, but what we give.

We don't reach true success, until we reach a point where we can help others. Steve Jobs and Walt Disney were not seen to be the most successful people because they created something brilliant and held onto it themselves.
They are seen as successful people because they created something brilliant that they knew had the power to change

millions of lives. It was only through the sharing of their creations that they found true success.

They had to first, want to create something new; then believe in it enough to turn it into an action and thirdly, they shared the success they already had with others.

If we have no ambition, we have no energy.

If we have no ambition, how will we succeed? How will we know when we have reached our goal?

Life without ambition is tiring. Life without energy is tiring. We try to find the easiest route, but we always end up at the same place, with the same decision to make.

Maybe it's time to accept our purpose, find our place and start living with the energy to do it.

It's like perpetual motion, without the up there is no down. Having too many ups in comparison to our downs means the perpetual motion slows down. Likewise, having too much weight without enough up-action cause to much resistance for the motion to continue with ease.

We will never survive the life we have.

No matter what we do, our life will end at some stage. What happens between now and then is our choice.

When we choose to discover, and invest in, our ambitions we find joy when they are accomplished.

When we experience this journey, we are then able to have the energy by finding purpose in all situations.

Joy is found when we appreciate the opportunities and purpose we are given.

This may take time to accomplish. It did for me. It is nothing short of a miracle that I am now writing this book. This is something I pushed against for a long time. Something that I thought someone else would do better than me. Someone who is more educated, who has more degrees and experience than me, but this is not their purpose, but mine. It took me a long time to accept that, and well, if I'm completely honest, I am still accepting this as part of my purpose.

I have found joy through this process.

Seeing the words come together on the page and hearing the feedback and the stories of change, brings me joy. Seeing the opportunities to learn, grow and share have been amazing to experience. When I started appreciating the opportunities that were given to me, my eyes were open to more.

Ambition past my lifetime.

My ambition is to live on past my lifetime. It's not that when I am no longer breathing, I will no longer be making a difference. It's not even that when my heart is no longer beating that people will remember my name. My ambition, my goal is that this world becomes a better place because I lived. I don't want to just give my children a childhood that they don't need to get over. I want to give my great, great, great grandchildren the opportunity to discover, live and grow into their best.

Chapter 13

Priorities

More than one ambition.

Chances are we may feel like we have more than one ambition. We don't just want to get the best job; we also want to have friends and build connection. Maybe have children, buy a house or some more land; we want to have success in more than one area of life.

This is why we need to know our priorities.

Unfortunately, we can't just write a list in order of the things we find most valuable. If we did this, we may have a spotless house, but no friends, or mountains of friends but a messy house. We could have amazing children but no life outside of them, or a busy social life but have little connection with our children.

It's good for our priorities to change.

Life would be boring if we did the same thing all the time, we would never make progress because we will only be doing what we've always done.
My priority on the weekend is not the same as it is during the week. My priorities while on holidays will change from being in the middle of a meeting.

Priorities are like seasons.

At any time our priorities will change, just like the seasons of life.
As teens, it may be finishing school, studying or finding a job. It may then become a partner or getting a promotion. Then our children may be our priority for a time, then they will be off, and our friends may be our priority.

Know what season of life we are in now.

Take time to discover where our ambitions are leading us, and what is the most balanced. This doesn't mean we focus solely on one thing until it is achieved, it means we allocate things according to the time required and the level of importance. Setting time aside for appreciating what we already have, achieving what we desire and celebrating our achievements.

It is important to know our priorities at any point in time.

If this means we have to write them down, then do it. Last thing at night, my priority is to tidy the house, so we can enjoy the mornings. My priority in the morning is checking in with my thoughts, helping me to be a better me for connections. My children are my priority at certain times of the day- as they wake up, our fun time and as I'm putting them to bed, and other times. They are not my top priority all the time. This doesn't mean that I don't run to their aid when I urgency calls, or I reject their need for conversation while I'm cooking dinner. It means I priorities our connection sometimes, and other times I have the opportunity to love them, learn from them and be there for them. This is them letting me know that they priorities our connection too. What this mean is that my value extends outside of one relationship.

My sole purpose is not relationships.

When my children were younger there was a time when that was all I had time for. Life was just getting by, trying to make them eat vegetable, pick their toys up or have a clean face.
In that season I appreciated that time, if I was to stay in those habits, I would have children who are not able to think for themselves and would probably hate me for trying to live their life.
If I was to always be checking up on my partner; wanting to know every thought and telling them mine, I assume

they would get sick of it fairly quickly because if my sole purpose was them, my purpose would be theirs. If my purpose was theirs, there would be no room for them and vice versa.

Our priorities are not comparable to others.

Our priority can't be to take what someone else has, or to be like someone else or to be where they are. We already have a priority. If being accepted by others is our sole priority, them being who we are and true to ourselves can't be. If being true to ourselves is our sole priority than building connections can't be.

My priority for a long time was to grow the positive in everyone. This meant combatting the negative action or thought and not against the person. It's good for us to create something new, not passing around the same bit of information but discover something new.

Take time to learn and to share.

Don't forget we first have to receive before we can give. Just remember that receiving isn't where joy is found, true giving is.

Prioritising our time.

Take time to study/learn/read, and time to show/share/explain.

Take time to exercise and enjoy our time being fit. Enjoy time cleaning, so you can enjoy time relaxing.

Enjoy investing in connections so we can enjoy the changes of life.

Priorities working together.

Schedules or routines are a great way to do this. Everyone knows what they need to do and what is expected of them, we are creating group habits. No one person has the sole responsibility, no one person can control a group as a whole. When the work is shared the benefits are shared. When the benefits are shared the joy is shared. Everyone has a part, knows their part and does their part. The best thing about working together is that we have the same time to relax together.

I used to dedicate one day to cleaning, and after a week at work that was the last thing I wanted to do. It's hard changing old habits and getting everyone on the same page, but once it is done, it's enjoyable. Now cleaning different areas on different days leaves time for relaxing weekends, catching up with friends, going away or anything else that becomes an opportunity.

Value the prepping to enjoy the moment.

It's spending time preparing dinner so we can eat it. We need to eat to sustain us. We need to communicate and invest in connections to enjoy life. If we don't enjoy cooking the food, we are less likely to enjoy the food. If we are not inquisitive about other people, we are less likely to enjoy our connection with them.

Understand the other side of the coin.

Knowing what is on the other side of the coin helps us to make our priorities. When we don't clean during the week, we enjoy the weekend less because we haven't been experiencing working together. Not working together means we need to spend energy re-establishing that habit within our connection. Breaking a connection of communication means less time enjoying the relationship and more time working on it.

When we look at the other side of the coin, the choice is easy.

Cleaning my house brings me joy. Those hard conversations, bring connection. Knowing my priorities brings me opportunities.

We see this in every situation. If a butterfly flapping its wings, on the other side of the earth can cause a tsunami; what habits do we have that fight against our connections. What is stealing our joy?

Putting the coins in place.

Knowing what is on the other side of the coin is important, but we have more than one coin. Just as the rich used to walk around with a sack full of coins, so can we. The wealth of life is not found in the number on our bank statement, but rather the amount of these coins that we have. Each coin has its own value. The cleaning coin is not as valuable as the partner one. The best friend coin is more valuable than the acquaintance one.

When faced with two or more opportunities, knowing the value of these coins, helps us to make clearer decisions. Understanding what is on the other side of each coin can help us to decide which choice is more valuable.

Prioritise the opportunities.

When we know what is in our coin bag, and when we understand their value, we can take each opportunity as it comes. Each time we have an opportunity to build a healthy connection, we will take it. In every moment we have the opportunity to reach out to someone; call someone, leave them a message or send them a gift.

Our priorities send us in different directions.

If we all had the same amount of time to live, if we were all born in the same place and time, given the same opportunities, our priorities would make us different.

Prioritising the preservation of humankind will not diminish our value as a person, but it will make this world a better place to be.

We all have the same amount of energy to use.

Our past investment of our energy has led to either its growth or decline. What we are choosing to prioritise from now on will become evident by the energy we have in the future. What are we prioritising now that is giving us positive energy, giving us positive connections, and giving us joy?

Chapter 14

Purpose

Our purpose is found in our joy.

Our purpose, the reason we are here, is not one sole purpose, one sole action, one moment or one decision. It is discovering our joy.

Our life is not a portrait but a collage.

When we look at our life as a picture, we can't see a portrait or a still life. There is no one moment in time that defines who we are. Our life is a collage, a compilation, a montage, or a patchwork. There is never just one thing happening in our lives, but many.

One word: purpose.

Sometimes when we ask or have conversations about our purpose, we look for a simple one word or one phrase to sum it up. We like to have it defined and organised so we can tick a box when we are done. We often have our purpose and our identity confused. What we are known for is not our sole purpose, but just one in the series of our life.

Instead of "What is my purpose?", ask "What am I purposed for?"

When we start asking this question, we start to see the opportunities we are given. We can come from a place of knowing we have an effect and choosing to make a positive effect, rather than trying to make any effect and hoping that it's good or will be good.

Opportunities bring purpose.

Knowing the purpose we have, in the opportunities we have been given, is investing our energy in a positive way. We appreciate what we have been giving and therefore appreciating the joy or rewards that come from them.

Our full purpose, or our full potential.

If we fully knew our purpose, we would know every step we would need to take, every conversation we would need to have and every decision we would need to make. We could not enjoy life or appreciate our connections as we would just be going through the motions.

Believe in our purpose.

Make a positive difference, however we make it. I have found the biggest hurdle in this life is knowing that I can make a difference. For years I wasn't living in my purpose for one reason, which is I didn't think I had one. I didn't think I could make a positive difference. I didn't think I could make my marriage better; I didn't think I could raise my children better. We can't give into a belief that we are not worth the opportunities we have been given.

Don't believe we can live our purpose without learning.

We will not live our purpose perfectly; we will not always have our priorities in order. We won't always know the value of our effect, but this is how we learn it. We learn what we value by the mistakes that we make. We spend time rebuilding the connections that we value more. Our purpose is not discovered, but created and crafted in every step we take, every conversation we have and every decision we make.

"Am I purposed for this?"

In every opportunity we can ask ourselves this question. Discover whether it fits us, or if it doesn't maybe we are meant to help someone else discover their purpose by letting them know of this opportunity.

The question isn't whether we have patience or not, it's how much we choose to exercise our patience.

By having connections and understanding our connections we live our purpose and help others to live their purpose. Patience is needed in the journey of life by understanding that we need to understand others. How much time are we willing to invest in understanding our own purpose and understanding the purpose of other's.

Measuring our purpose.

We can measure our patience by measuring the times we are living in our purpose. If we are taking each situation as it comes and am taking the opportunities that we are given, we will be enjoying life. Not enjoying a moment but enjoying all of life. When we are enjoying our lives and living in our purpose, impatience has no place in our life.

By straggling against patience, we destroy it.

Know the battle we are fighting by knowing who our enemy is. When we think patience is our enemy, we are fighting against ourselves. When we understand that lack of understanding is the enemy, we can choose to put away the doubt and make or continue to make a choice. By sowing into our purpose, understanding our priorities and knowing what we want to achieve, impatience has nowhere to stand.

Life has the purpose that we give it.

Life isn't something that we do once, and it is done. Purpose is not something we can box up and be free once it is complete. Our purpose is to sustain life, we sustain life by enjoying it.

Being part way patient, is not an option.

Only being patient until we get what we want, or until a certain point, is not patience at all. Let patience have its full work in our lives.

At moments of impatience, we can look for our purpose. What are we not understanding and what are we purposed for in this moment?

Chapter 15

Understanding Perseverance

Patience is the coming together of all these things.

To have complete patience we need to understand the triad that makes up patience.

That is:
Choice,
Opportunity,
Desire.

Miss one of these and we no longer have patience.

The first point and the consistent one is choice. We always have a choice, and no one can take that away from us.

The second is Opportunity. Opportunities are always there but they may not look like we expect them to.

And the third point in Desire. Our desires relate to our deepest needs. They are found in our purpose or our ambition. Desire is not related in any way to fear, pride, shame or blame. Our desire has to come from our unique experience, perspective and purpose within a community.

Choose self-discipline.

Self-discipline is needed when we have the opportunity but not the desire, or when we have the desire but not the opportunity.

Patience is our opportunity.

Patience is knowing our purpose is not limited by time. It's knowing that if we have a pure desire, the opportunity will come. If we have an opportunity and 'know' what we need, the desire will come.

Patience is relationships.

Sometimes we have the opportunity but not the desire. This goes for exercising, working, schooling, writing and a million other opportunities we have in one day. Every morning we get out of bed, we have an opportunity. Every day we go to work, school or play, we continue to grow. As we continue to grow our desire will continue to grow.

Exercise is the evidence of this example.

If we have ever been unhealthy, tired, sick or hurt, we didn't jump up and say "Yes, I get to run/train/swim (exercise)". I know that has been all of us at some stage. Even pro-athletes and the fittest people I know don't always desire to do what they do. They choose to do it because they know it's the best thing for them. They know that as they continue to do it, they will get fitter, and it will get easier. On the days when we are sick, tired or hurting, we can continue to stick to our habit, our routines and it will get easier.

Giving up is squashing the desire for anything to come.

Sometimes we have a desire for promotion, for learning or to befriend that person but we don't have the opportunity. When we choose to keep that desire and not squash it, even though it hurts, even though we don't know how and even though it seems crazy and doesn't make sense to anyone else, we need to keep that pure desire. Knowing that if we keep it, an opportunity will come.

When we have a desire for a promotion, we generally don't turn up on our first day of work and ask for one. The opportunity of the promotion is coming closer the more that we acknowledge the desire for it. When we have a desire for promotion, getting to work early is easy, giving our best or doing that little extra work becomes an easy choice. Although the opportunity for the promotion is not evident just yet, we take the opportunities we have to work towards our desire. When, through the passage of time we are given the opportunity, the choice has formerly been made.

Sometimes it's a little less evident.

Such as befriending that person at work or communicating with a person, we can't explain why we feel like we need to know that person, but we do. It's not just the picture or the comment but something else. We can't work towards that desire like the promotion, as we won't be able to see the change or opportunity happening. As we trust the process and the positive intentions we have, we continue to be open to the opportunities we have and invest into that desire.

Choose between wanting and not having or wanting and never having.

We need to make the choice between; squashing the desire that make us unique as individuals or, continuing with the desire even though it's hard, even though it hurts, even though we don't understand everything. Giving up on our unique purpose is giving up on our life.

It will always lead to a place of searching.

If we fear running out of time, we waste time by trying to know everything or please everyone. Another opportunity to learn and change will come, all we can do is enjoy the opportunities we are given. No need to worry about the things to come, but to look forward to them. Our life has a time limit on it, we have little control over the time we have, all we have control over is how we invest it. Use it wisely, not spending it worrying about how we spend it, but spending it with joy in our hearts and adventure on our minds.

We are not going to run out of time.

The time frame we are given, is not dictated by a list we need to accomplish or by things we need to know. Our time is dictated by the value we give to it. I have known of 12-year-old girl who has had a greater impact on the world than men who live till their 90's.

What will it cost?

The price of our life is death. This we are guaranteed. What we can control is how much of our own pride are we willing to sacrifices for a better life.

We have each been given a time to live.

This time is for none of us to know in advance. It's for none of us to claim the day we are to be born. We are not given anything but the time we have.

A wise choice for the time we have.

We can only choose between protecting our lives knowing that we will fail, for one day we will all die; or enjoying our lives hoping that one day we might live on through the gifts given to the hearts of others.

Perseverance Summary

Giving up only makes it harder.

Work towards something.

Achievements sustain energy; energy sustains achievements.

Our choice is between enjoying and protecting.

Our purpose is found in our pure desires.

The value we give to life, is the value we are given by life.

I consistently keep my priorities in perspective.

References

Research
The Bible (NKJV, NIV, NKJ)
Oxford dictionary
dictionary.com

Influential Books
Raising a Secure Child,
The Power of a Praying Wife,
The Daniel Dilemma,

Code= UCP

Other influences
Using my life as an experiment, I am living nine months without expectations. Breaking down of old frame works and ideas. The responses and reactions I have received have been a measuring staff to the acceptance of other. I have met many new people who have all influenced me during this time and during my journey. The struggles I have been through with children and business has allowed me to understand that real authority doesn't have to yell or make demands. Real authority comes through a unified cause, an insistence of doing what is not only right for me, but what is the best for everyone.

www.ingramcontent.com/pod-product-compliance
Lightning Source LLC
Chambersburg PA
CBHW072006290426
44109CB00018B/2148